I Want to Make a Difference

Discover your purpose in life and change things for the better

Tim Drake

CYAN

Marshall Cavendish
Editions

Copyright © 2006 Tim Drake

First published in 2006 by:

Marshall Cavendish Editions
An imprint of Marshall Cavendish International (Asia) Private Limited
A member of Times Publishing Limited
Times Centre, 1 New Industrial Road
Singapore 536196
T: +65 6213 9300
F: +65 6285 4871
E: te@sg.marshallcavendish.com
Online bookstore: www.marshallcavendish.com/genref

and

Cyan Communications Limited
119 Wardour Street
London W1F 0UW
United Kingdom
T: +44 (0)20 7565 6120
E: sales@cyanbooks.com
www.cyanbooks.com

A CIP record for this book is available from the British Library

ISBN-13 978 981 261 831 3 (Asia & ANZ)
ISBN-10 981 261 831 7 (Asia & ANZ)
ISBN 1-904879-63-2 (Rest of world)

Printed and bound in Singapore

To Lizzie—wonderful wife, and mother, who nurses three days a week, but gives continuously for seven, and the role model of a Beneficial Presence difference maker.

Contents

CONTENTS

Acknowledgments

I would like to thank Lizzie, Lettice, and David for valuable help with proofreading, and especially Tansy for proofreading and many insightful suggestions. I would also like to thank Miles Protter of The Values Partnership for sharing his thoughts on values, and the team at The Future Foundation for access to research and thoughts on other sources of information.

Preface

When our daughter Lettice was three, she loved drawing faces. Like most parents, we enjoyed praising her efforts.

One day, she showed us her drawing of a face, which was recognizable as such, but had no eyes. "That's wonderful, Lettice," I said. "But where are the eyes?"

She gave me a look that children reserve for parents who are being particularly stupid. She held up her pencil, and said, "Here. In my pencil."

Discovering our purpose, and learning to be more effective at making a difference, is about engaging more positively with the world around us, both to make things better, and to release our potential for the fulfillment that we keep locked up in our pencils.

All that is necessary for the triumph of evil is that good men do nothing.

Edmund Burke

1

What is the Make a Difference Mindset, and why is it important?

WHAT IT IS

"I want to make a difference." How often do we hear people say that? And how often do we say it ourselves?

Most of us want to make a difference. The trouble is, we aren't too sure how to do it. More importantly, we're not totally clear why we want to make a difference.

We have a feeling that we are here for a purpose, but we're not too sure what that purpose is. We believe we should be doing something about it, but we're not sure what. We feel we want to leave our mark on the world—some trace of our passing—but we're confused as to what sort of mark it might be.

So the desire to make a difference exists in a kind of vacuum. We know it's intrinsically worthwhile, but it's still floating around on some wish list, not yet written down or prioritized.

It's our goal to make a difference, but we probably won't get round to it this week.

This book is about two things. First, it is about the Make a Difference Mindset, which is a simple action plan to make us more effective at making a difference in our chosen domain. Second, and possibly more importantly, it is about how we can discover our purpose. Discovering our purpose will enable us to find where and how we will make a difference, as well as tap into the energy source for our drive and enthusiasm to make it happen.

Through making a difference, we can find fulfillment. Through discovering, and living, our purpose, we can find freedom. We can unlock our enthusiasm and passion, because our lives will begin to have meaning. Finding meaning makes it much easier to turn up to work that has become a chore, go home to a challenging family situation, or take on and resolve difficulties in our social life.

One of the benefits of finding our purpose, and having meaning in our lives, is that fulfillment is more achievable than happiness. Happiness is tricky. It comes and goes, and is hard to sustain when things get tough. Things getting tough, however, taken as part of the rich tapestry of life in which we are encountering a difficult patch, can be fulfilling. So fulfillment is achievable, and more enduring, than happiness. It's not only more achievable; it's more satisfying and worthwhile.

Let's look first at the Mindset.

The Make a Difference Mindset is the deliberate, conscious, decision to make a positive difference. Either to the people around us, or the situation in which we find ourselves. The Mindset defines the move from generalized drift to a voyage with a clear goal. It creates an unshakable inner confidence that we can change things for the better. It confirms our wish to leave a legacy, either in improving the lives of those we are close to, and come into contact with, or in changing the way organizations or societies behave.

And it gives us the energy to do so.

The Make a Difference Mindset moves what is now probably an occasional unconscious competence into a regular conscious competence. Our currently sporadic ability to make a difference becomes less haphazard and random.

Note: the Make a Difference Mindset is complementary to any religious or spiritual faith, understanding, or commitment you may have. It works in conjunction with it, and does not replace it in any way.

DIFFERENCE DRIVERS, DIFFERENCE DELIVERERS, AND BENEFICIAL PRESENCES

The differences we can make tend to polarize into two types. The first is the humanitarian response to suffering in all its forms. The second is the moral response to perceived failures by governmental, non-governmental, or commercial organizations to behave with integrity or compassion, or to respond with energy to the environmental challenges facing our planet. The first would include response to famines in foreign lands, or the homeless on our doorstep. The second includes response to an organization that bullies and manipulates its workers or suppliers, or ignores its responsibilities to the environment.

Making a difference is a very broad church. It involves bringing our humanity to bear in order to positively benefit people, organizations, our society, and future generations. Good things happen which probably wouldn't have happened without the contribution of the individual attempting to make a difference. On an individual level, making a difference can be as simple as being compassionate to another human being at a time of need.

> In essence, it is a desire to improve the lot of our fellow man or woman, to an extent that reflects how ambitious we are, and how effective we are at influencing events or making things happen.

The people who make differences on a societal scale we can call Difference Drivers (often aided by Difference Deliverers), and the people who make personal, often one-to-one, differences we'll call Beneficial Presences.

There are, of course, gradations in between, but the distinction between the three types lies in the focus of purpose and ambition. Difference Drivers intend to make waves, and change paradigms. They intend to make the world a different and a better place. They want to leave a legacy, and they want that legacy to be in the public domain.

The **Difference Drivers** tilt at windmills, and sometimes they knock the windmills over. They find a situation in the organization they work for, the community they are part of, or the society they live in, that jars with their personal values, and they set out to change it.

As we shall see later, some of the great pioneering charities—like Amnesty International and Greenpeace—have been started by an individual, and subsequently a group of individuals (Difference Deliverers), who have been imbued with a sense of purpose that has made them passionate antagonists of the status quo.

Passionate antagonists of the status quo are the chief source of Difference Drivers. They are not always easy people to have around. Even Nelson Mandela, who evolved into a serene Beneficial Presence, was once a Difference Driver, and his weapons were guns and bombs.

Difference Deliverers are the people who consciously set out to make a difference, and do so. Though the individual act or acts can at times seem small, their contribution to the overall impact can be vital. The small acts of the Difference Deliverers can cumulatively make a massive impact. Most of us fit into this category.

This difference can be in supporting Difference Drivers. It is very rarely that social change is accomplished by one person working alone. You can't start a movement for change without having people in that movement.

Sometimes these helpful foot soldiers can be just as brave and committed as the Difference Driver him or herself. Lech Walesa, the visionary leader of the freedom movement in Poland, which was instrumental in the final toppling of Communism in that country and subsequently Eastern Europe, was a shop steward in the shipyards. It took courage for him to stand up and resist an ugly, authoritarian regime, but it took just as much courage for the individual shipyard workers in Gdansk to resist the soldiers and secret police coercing them back to work. It was these Difference Deliverers who ultimately made the difference.

Most Difference Deliverers, however, operate individually, or in small teams. The differences that they make are important, whether they are on the level of family, job, community, distinct groups in need of succor or support, or on a societal level. The differences they make may only be relatively small, but cumulatively the difference can be huge, and immensely worthwhile.

Beneficial Presences are people who make a difference through living who they are. Their purpose is to love and cherish other human beings, and they gain their meaning from compassion for, or service to, others. They add huge value to other human beings just by making them feel valued. Some are just natural servers, or are naturally compassionate, others have to work at it.

The legacy they leave is usually in the private domain. They are loved by those around them. When they die, their funerals often see mourners turn up in large numbers, most of whom do no know each other, and who had no idea the person they are mourning touched so many lives. They are sometimes revered, but are usually not aware of it. Their reward is in personal fulfillment, not changing the world.

On the other hand, some Beneficial Presences have no one at their funeral. This may be because they made a profound difference to someone who suffered prolonged incapacity or illness, to the exclusion of all else. Their hugely generous act of dedicating their life to another human being meant they couldn't touch the lives of other human beings, because all their energies had to be focused on helping just one person. Yet for that one person, whom they helped and nursed, they made a pivotal difference.

The aim of this book is simple. It is to help you decide whether you want to be a Difference Driver, a Difference Deliverer, or a Beneficial Presence, and in what domain in your life you want to start. Once you have decided, it will help you get better at making a difference. You'll get better at it by coming to understand what is often very elusive—your purpose. Having found meaning in what you are setting out to achieve, you will develop some specific techniques which will make you more effective at delivering the difference. The exciting part of your journey will then begin—making it happen.

WHY IT'S IMPORTANT

Thomas Hobbes in *Leviathan* describes man's existence as nasty, brutish, and short. He was in fact discussing man's existence in times of war, but the phrase resonates so powerfully today, because it seems at times that we are living in a period of constant war. Not just in the conventional sense, but in the sense of society reeling out of control, with anger and gratuitous violence filling our newspapers and television screens on a daily basis.

The ubiquity of messages indicating near-anarchy in societies around the world, from West to East, makes it all too easy to fall into a slough of despondency. This despondency can negatively affect our ability to make a difference, and build a better tomorrow.

Pessimism reduces both our vision of what is possible, and our ability to change things for the better. It is all around us, and it has an insidious appeal. The media—24-hour television news and the right-leaning press in particular— tend to demonize and over-simplify complex social change. They look for easy—and usually negative— angles on events, and exclude most of what is positive.

The reality, however, is somewhat different. The negative presentation of our global society distorts what is actually happening. Let me be clear. I am not for one moment suggesting that there are not some extremely sad and distressing things going on in societies all round the world. There are huge challenges facing us as we proceed in the twenty-first century.

What I am saying is that the lens through which we look at things is distorted. Yet the distortion is so pervasive that it threatens to become a self-fulfilling prophecy. In the next chapter I put forward evidence that because more and more of us want to make a difference, we are approaching a tipping point, at which the people looking to influence things positively will outnumber the negative and inactive members of society.

At this point—or soon afterwards—the pressure of this dominant group in society will start to have significant influence on how corporations, organizations, and governments behave. That influence will be positive, and is likely to combine with another emerging theme—that of citizens, consumers, and employees (the same people wearing different hats) demanding more direct and democratic involvement in major decision making.

Let us first examine some of the origins of our pessimism, and the wounds that it inflicts upon us, so that having identified it, we can overcome it.

POSTMODERNISM AND ALL THAT NONSENSE

Postmodernism has a lot to answer for. The term itself is loose and slippery, and tends to summarize the black mood of despair at the evolution of civilization, which underpins the editorials of many newspapers today. To over-simplify for the sake of brevity, postmodernism is the label (devised initially by some French intellectuals) applied in the later part of the twentieth century to the state of near-chaos which they perceived society had reached.

They argued that the confidence of the Enlightenment (which for the last 200 years or so has discerned an increasing power of reason over ignorance, order over disorder, and science over superstition) was misplaced, and wrong. We, as a society were not evolving at all, and the idea of the progress of civilization was wrong.

They further argued that the underpinnings of the so-called meta-narratives (world views like Christianity, Marxism, Islam, and so on), had fostered a belief that humanity had the capacity to improve its lot, and that this belief was a false one. Nazism, Stalinism, neo-colonialism, racism, and Third World hunger were adduced as just a few of the reasons that modernism (the progressive evolution of an improving society) was a shattered theory, which, they argued, should therefore be replaced by postmodernism.

Postmodernism is not too clear what it does stand for, but is very clear on what it rejects—that is, any concept of society improving or progressing in any way. Furthermore, postmodernists see individuals as corks tossed on a sea of change, unable to affect outcomes in any meaningful way. Zygmunt Bauman, one of the most trenchant writers on postmodernism, describes its "all-deriding, all-eroding, all-dissolving destructiveness," pointing out that it "braces itself for a life without truths, standards and ideals."

Intellectuals exist to challenge the shibboleths of conventional thought, and I'm all for that. Postmodernism, however, has bred a de-energized defeatism that negates responsibility and wallows in its own negativity. Pessimism is a powerful force that attracts people of all ages and backgrounds. It is fashionable, and it is enervating, because, like the feelings of depression it engenders, it develops what Charles Leadbeater, in the excellent and uplifting *Up The Down Escalator*, calls "learned helplessness." Pessimists become so used to the idea that they are helpless, that they believe it, even when it is not true.

Pessimists learn to see themselves as victims of circumstances that are beyond their control. This helplessness becomes a self-fulfilling prophecy, and paralysis of will sets in. The *apparent* crumbling of the major psychological supports (religion, the state, the family) compounds their sense of individual isolation, vulnerability, and inability to cope on their own.

If we want to make a positive difference, we need to unlearn helplessness pretty quickly. To do so, let's consider some of the facts.

2

The good news: the positive difference makers are winning

Two major political changes that have taken place in my lifetime, both of which go directly contrary to the postmodern theory of degeneration and chaos. The end of the Cold War and the collapse of apartheid in South Africa are major world-changing events, both overwhelmingly positive. As a result of the ending of the Cold War, freedom has been given to millions of people who had never known it, and had little expectation of seeing it in their lifetimes.

This is confirmed by research from the World Bank, which indicates that between 1980 and 2000 the number of authoritarian regimes in the world fell from 70 to 30. Freedom House, the global democracy advocate, tells us that in 1980 there were 54 countries which had multiparty elections and some element of formal democracy. These 54 countries accounted for 46 percent of world population. Today, using the same criteria, 121 countries, accounting for over 80 percent of world population, are democratic.

Even Africa is improving in terms of democratic accountability. According to the *Economist*, since the end of the Cold War, 18 rulers have already been voted out of office. In the 1960s and 1970s, none had been.

Let's take the UK as an example of what has been happening in the Western world—and latterly in the Asia–Pacific. Since the 1950s, real incomes have risen by 400 percent. The affluence of UK citizens has been augmented by house price rises that have given great swathes of the population access to capital for the first time. We are healthier, live longer—and importantly—live younger. We work in cleaner, safer jobs, which by and large are more interesting and have a lower element of drudgery. We behave and think like people 20 or 30 years younger, had we lived in our parents' generation.

We are more mobile (we travel on average 30 miles a day, as against 3 in 1950, not to mention foreign holidays and weekend excursions), we are better educated, and with the Internet, and an active and penetrating media, certainly better informed. We are more self-confident and assertive. We are far more tolerant of, and often welcoming to, diversity of all kinds (which if you belong to a minority group of whatever description is positively life-changing).

The class system is discredited, and for the most part is gasping its last breaths. There are more opportunities for all, and for the young, there are unprecedented chances to travel and see other cultures. The development of lifelong learning means that we have more affordable access to quality teaching of a fantastic range of subjects and crafts.

We have choice in financial services. Instead of going on one knee to get a loan that charged usurious rates, we can now pick and choose—and change—at will.

We have choice in food shopping. The variety—and low price—of foods in the supermarkets is of a richness and depth that would have staggered us just 20 years ago, let alone 30 or 40. We have a huge choice in media: terrestrial, cable, and satellite television, and a mass of digital radio stations and magazines that cover every taste and interest group you can imagine. Not to mention the Aladdin's cave of choice opening up through mobile telephony.

The willful ignoring of theses positive changes by most commentators, and the negative spin put on all changes in our society, are what the Future Foundation, a research organization and consultancy specializing in current and future global trends, call **The Myth of Decline**. They analyze a whole raft of commonly accepted "truths" on the declining standards in society, and demonstrate them to be false. They expose the myths—a tide of rising crime (in fact it's declining), massive rises in alcohol consumption and drunkenness in Europe (overall it's static, and has declined 40 percent in France) and so on.

One of the team at Future Foundation, Peter Wilmott, author and family psychologist, puts it this way, "It's a myth it was better then and a myth it is worse now." He highlights the so-called decline in the family as a unit, and the decline in family values. In fact, the family is growing in importance as a unit, and as a "psychological lynchpin."

The so-called "parenting deficit"—today's busy, two-job, work focused parents devoting less time to their children—is demonstrably untrue. In reality, today's parents have fewer children, and they are spending an average of 85 minutes per day—per child—concentrating on childcare—a whole lot more than the 25 minutes per day spent in the 1970s. Part of this is due to the parents' fears (again largely not fact-based) of letting children play on their own in the garden or in the road.

On family values the research indicates that, if anything, they are strengthening. The family unit is changing somewhat—some people define their closest friends, along with their children, partners, and parents as close family. The relationships between middle-aged adults (both male and female) and their parents are getting closer (helped by the ubiquity of mobile phones), as are the relationships between grandparents and grandchildren.

The myth of decline is an international phenomenon. US sociologist Barry Glassner writes in *The Culture of Fear*:

> Why are so many fears in the air, and so many of them unfounded? Why, as crime rates plunged throughout the 1990s, did two thirds of Americans think they were soaring? How did it come about that by mid-decade 62 percent of us described ourselves as "truly desperate" about crime—almost twice as many as in the late 1980s when crime rates were higher?

He continues, "Give us a happy ending and we write a new disaster story."

So the decline in quality of life, and what is called social capital, is largely a myth. Despite that, and the overwhelming positive progress on many fronts, the pessimists do have some legitimate grouses to get upset about. Sadly, being pessimists, they get upset, rather than making any positive contribution to their improvement.

Yes, there is a downside to how our society is evolving. We are searching for moral certainty. It would be helpful to recapture some of the lost notion of piety. The traditional idea of piety was that we should profoundly respect nature, individual human beings—however weak or unattractive—our history, and the institutions of our community.

Piety comes from the Roman word *pietas*, meaning respect for parents and ancestors, for law and civil order, for the inherited framework of civilized life. The rapid changes in our society are in many ways invigorating, and too much respect can be stultifying and dangerous (look at totalitarian regimes) but an absolute absence of piety is also dangerous. A lack of reverence for people and for nature can lead to a fragile, self-centered society that lacks a moral compass.

This leads people to respect personality—the surface of human beings—rather than character—their inner worth. This in turn leads to the cult of celebrities, rather than heroes. As a result we countenance vulgarity and exhibitionism that continually plumbs new depths. (Now there's a cause for the pessimist newspapers to take some positive action on—a campaign to take celebrities off their pages, and find some heroes instead.)

Another failure of our society—despite some politicians' serious efforts—is to have allowed an underclass to develop. The underclass is too far adrift from the rest of the population in terms of income, education, health, and hope. This is inexcusable, deeply worrying, and needs to be urgently addressed by government.

But we are a very long way from a moral vacuum. Anyone who spends any time around teenagers will know that they have a powerfully developed sense of fairness. Teenagers are on the front line of the moral hotspots—sexism, racism, globalization, and the environment. They work as individuals, and in networked collaboration, to fight for their beliefs, many of which are as least as idealistic and worthwhile as anything fought for in the 1960s.

The point is that action is needed, not moaning. The problem with pessimism is that it builds barricades and fortresses to hide behind, which shut the mind down, and with it, our energy to take action. These barricades and fortresses shelter a comforting, reactionary, delusive view of the past as a place where everyone was nice, white, didn't take drugs, only drank in moderation, was always polite, and lived a happy rural life in a village.

In reality, nowadays most of us live in cities. The multiplicity and diversity of culture—food, theatre, dance—you name it—gives a fantastic richness to our lives, not available behind a barricade. And for those minorities historically marginalized and oppressed—homosexuals, Jews, blacks, women, dissidents and the whole panoply of eccentrics and oddballs—life is full of new promise. In cities, they can be themselves, and have pride in their difference.

People have said to my wife Lizzie and me over the years, "How can you bring up kids in a big city?" The answer is—with great pleasure. The excitement, the energy, the access to some of the best cultural experiences in the world, is a huge privilege for them, and for us.

PESSIMISTS CAN'T HACK IT

This is the essence of it. Encouraged by the media's false picture of the world we live in, pessimists tend to feel helpless, and out of control in an environment that is negative and deteriorating.

They follow the lead of the media they read, and take refuge in complaining. Their negative mindset is the manifestation of the Islamic saying:

> A thankful person is thankful under all circumstances. A complaining soul complains, even if he lives in paradise.

Psychological studies over the years indicate that pessimists tend to achieve less, give up more easily, and get depressed more quickly and more frequently.

Optimists, on the other hand, tend to achieve more at school, in sport, at work, and in life generally. They also tend to live longer, have better health, and recover more quickly from illness. They are more creative, and even if their brain tells them it can't be done, their heart tells them it can.

Landing on the moon, running the mile in four minutes, sailing round the world single-handed, building a business from scratch, setting up a charity to help the underprivileged or the oppressed, helping—in a small or a large way—people who are struggling in life, are all things that need an optimistic outlook to undertake. A pessimist would be unlikely to set out to fight the odds to succeed.

I know from personal experience how disempowering pessimism can be. If I suffer a very brief spell of pessimism, and some obstacle is put in my path to something I am trying to achieve, my immediate reaction is to consider giving up. The energy seeps away, and I feel a powerful sense of inertia taking over.

I quickly recover, even more determined to succeed, but the experience of a desire to capitulate, and take the easy, inactive route out, is a powerful one. This underlines the importance of what Stephen Covey, one of the best writers and teachers on personal development, calls the necessity to "carry your own weather around with you."

Carrying your own weather around with you means having a well-developed and grounded self-esteem that enables you to sustain your own feeling of positive wellbeing through the ups and downs of daily life. Doug Hooper, who worked with life prisoners in some of the toughest gaols in the United States, gives a telling example of what I'm talking about.

He was walking along the pavement one morning with a friend, who stopped to buy a newspaper at a newsstand. There was a short queue, and Hooper was surprised to see how rude and surly the newsvendor was to all his customers. When it came to his friend's turn to buy his paper, he saw his friend behaving as his natural, charming and friendly self, despite the vendor's gratuitous offensiveness.

As they walked away, Hooper, astonished, asked his friend why he was so positive and friendly in the face of such boorish behavior. His friend replied, "You don't think I'm going to let a bum like that affect how I feel, do you?"
The fact is that most of us do.

Carrying our own weather around with us is a prerequisite for becoming successful at making a difference. There are plenty of bums around who want to make life smaller and more negative for us. They cannot be allowed to blacken our mood, or diminish our energy level.

MORE OF US ARE IN A POSITION TO MAKE A DIFFERENCE

The consistent rise in affluence over the past 20 or so years in large parts of the globe has meant that most of us are progressing up Maslow's hierarchy of needs. The hierarchy was devised by the psychologist Abraham Maslow some 50 or 60 years ago to explain the evolution and development of human motivation. His basic argument was that once needs are satisfied they no longer motivate. So you can be extremely thirsty, but once you have found a tap and slaked your thirst, water is no longer very motivating for you.

Published in 1949, it has five steps. The bottom step is physiological needs (hunger, thirst, sex, excretion, and so on); the second is security (self-preservation, safety); the third is social, or belonging (acceptance, membership, team spirit, and so on); the fourth is ego (self-respect, importance, dignity); and the top step is self-actualization (achievement, development, creativity, and helping others).

Interestingly he later developed it further, and changed the top step, by repositioning it as an active state—"self-actualizing"—not a passive state—"self-actualization." The reason for this was that he felt that we never finally arrive at our goal of fulfillment, only reach important stages on a continuous journey.

Self-actualizing means searching for meaning, giving service to others, and generally making a difference in some way for the benefit of humanity. So moving up the hierarchy means developing as a human being, from covering the basic requirements for life, through the need to satisfy our ego (recognition) to the need to help others find their fulfillment.

Some people, of course, never reach the higher levels, and often they can't see why anyone else would want to either. What is interesting, however, is that these people, if they are financially successful in life, often end up being major donors to charities. They are striving to get recognition for being essentially good people (whatever their behavior on the way up), and understand that the only true qualification for being good is to give service to others.

Moving up the higher levels of the hierarchy—and understanding why and how to make a difference—requires personal growth. The phrase "personal growth" is a difficult one, and capable of many definitions.

What I mean by personal growth is the strategic development of our potential as human beings. Crucial in this is the building of a well-grounded self-esteem. It is crucial, because in today's flatter social structures, where democracy is taking over from command-and-control hierarchies, the ability to cope with personal rejection is an almost daily requirement.

Respect for rank, authority, position, or wealth has dwindled over the years, especially in Western societies. In many ways this has been a good thing, because deference for authority was often built on position, not worth. The bosses and rulers were safe from dissent or criticism, because their position in a rigid hierarchy demanded that what they said was obeyed. Their ability or worth as individuals had little to do with it.

As these command and control systems of social organization evolve into more democratic, egalitarian ones, position is no longer a guarantee of authority. Decisions of leaders are questioned, and if found wanting, are ignored or disobeyed.

What this means is that no one is safe. Those in authority can be told they have feet of clay, or to take a jump. Managers, schoolteachers, politicians, police officers, religious leaders, all have to expect to cope with rejection in one form or another. Those who can retain their humanity, warmth, composure, and good humor while establishing their authority deservedly become respected leaders. They build respect with the people they are dealing with, as well as building their own self-esteem.

The personal development required to achieve this authority and ability to lead others is a subject I will address in more depth later. For the present, suffice it to say that Maslow put his finger on the heart of it, when he said, "Every day we have a thousand choices, between safety and growth." As we make our unsteady way up the hierarchy of needs, we take one step forwards, and sometimes two steps back.

Growth means getting out of our comfort zone, taking risks, and trying to cope with new challenges to our sense of self. Safety means taking no risks, continuing to believe our own propaganda about ourselves, and not knowing if we could have coped, had we put our heads over the parapet.

Figures on the speed at which we as a society are moving up Maslow's hierarchy are hard to come by. We all have anecdotal evidence of the significant growth in search for justice, fairness, significance, the desire to make a difference, which make up the higher levels of the hierarchy. A recent study by the retail arm of a large management consultancy showed that high up in the scores for what shoppers were looking for in the shopping experience was "meaning." By this they meant that the perceived values of the retailers they chose to shop in chimed with their own sense of what was right, fair, and just. Ten years ago meaning wouldn't even have been on the radar screen, let alone in the beam of the headlights.

One small numerical handle we have on it is through another version of Maslow's hierarchy, developed by commercial consultancies. This is a three-level hierarchy, dividing the population by values and behavior into Sustenance Driven/Survivors, Outer Directeds, and Inner Directeds. The first group is self-explanatory. The Outer Directeds are motivated by conspicuous consumption and status. They gain their self-esteem from what other people think of them. It is important to them what car they drive, what job they have, and whether their kids think they are cool or not.

The Inner Directeds (the equivalent of the Self-Actualizers) are more experimental, and are concerned by social values, and making a difference. They include older idealists, and younger groups active in social and political causes. What they feel about things is what is important, not what other people think. To over-simplify, Outer Directeds are worried about what the boss thinks of what they are doing, whereas the Inner Directeds are worried about what future generations will think of what they are doing.

In a 1998 study by Synergy Consulting, the percentage of Inner Directeds was put at 25 percent of the population. A forecast by Kinsman, looking at the split in 2020, puts the percentage at 40–50 percent.

Even if the Kinsman forecast of 40–50 percent of our society being inner-values driven is on the high side, which it may be, the thought that getting on for half the population by 2020 could be looking to help others, and to make a difference, is both exciting and uplifting. Not only does it bode well for how business and governments will need to behave, it could be a significant positive step for the future of the planet.

So there are many reasons to be optimistic about the evolving economic and social context.

There are plenty of challenges too, but challenges are food and drink to the person wanting to make a difference. In a confusing and uncertain world we are looking for leadership and guidance, but at the same time we are becoming far clearer in our thinking about what principles and values will underpin that current and future world. Difference Drivers and Difference Deliverers, with their optimism and sense of purpose, will be well equipped to play an important role in defining those principles and providing that leadership.

There is more and growing evidence that this is already happening. Not only are some of the corrupt and violent forces receding (apartheid and the dehumanizing grimness of communist ideologies), they are beginning to be replaced by the forces of enlightenment and human dignity.

Political correctness is such a force. It is much mocked, but it has delivered huge benefits to those whose protection it sought to provide. It has restored human dignity to minorities whose ethnic, religious, or sexual orientation used to be the constant butt of humor or abuse. Irish jokes, Polish jokes, Belgian jokes—or whoever was the neighboring country chosen to be parodied as being stupid, greedy, or tight-fisted— are much reduced in many societies.

THE GROWTH AND EVOLUTION OF VOLUNTEERING

A mounting body of research into social beliefs and behaviors is showing important changes in our aspirations. These changes are fundamental, and would have been hard to predict just 10 or 20 years ago.

What is interesting—and significant—is that intangible, rather than tangible, aspirations are now becoming huge drivers of behavior. Rather than a larger house, a bigger car, or a bigger pay packet, the biggest motivator now is personal fulfillment. It's no longer what you own, but what you *do*—together with family, friends, or in the community—that is important. This desire for fulfillment, coupled with *how* you live your life, starts to put the wish to make a difference—to positively impact on events and people— more and more center stage.

This is manifesting itself in the increase in volunteering. When Margaret Thatcher pronounced society dead in the 1980s, it seemed that the deeply unattractive, financially dominated, "me first and the devil take the hindmost" attitudes she seemed to promulgate and encourage were set to take over as the norms in UK society.

Fortunately, it has turned out very differently. The growth in volunteering has been exciting and significant for some years now. By 2003 *The Citizenship Survey* from the UK government shows 17 million people in England and Wales taking part in some sort of volunteering activity. This was 1.7 million higher than the previous level in 2001.

As a proportion of the active population, the percentage of people active in their communities rose from 48 percent in 2001 to 51 percent in 2003. Within this figure, the most exciting growth was in those participating at least once a month—the regular volunteers, who are serious about doing something to make a difference.

So whatever the pessimists may be saying about society falling apart, over half the population aren't listening to their siren voices, and allowing fragmentation to become a self-fulfilling prophecy. They are getting off their backsides, and doing something to make a difference.

The whole volunteering movement has been greatly encouraged by businesses, which see local communities as important stakeholders (the source of both employees, and to a lesser extent, customers). Recognizing their responsibility to the communities they operate in, and the need to be attractive to current and potential staff, many businesses run match time schemes.

These schemes allow employees to claim up to 40 hours of paid time to do voluntary work. Some companies, like Timberland (the footwear company) even include active engagement in the community in their personal and management development schemes. They find it a two-way win. The employees benefit from and enjoy the engagement in helping the community, and the firm benefits from more motivated, energetic staff, and strong team building amongst those taking part.

This felicitous interconnectedness between business and its wider stakeholders in the community could be supercharged once more metrics are developed to quantify the benefits of such activity. Measurable benefits might include increases in staff retention, increased staff morale, decrease in formal training costs, more effective team working, the cross-fertilization of ideas, and new approaches to innovation.

Evidence is also emerging that volunteering keeps you young. Numerous studies confirm that volunteering into old age enhances both physical and psychological health, and lowers rates of depression and mortality.

Yes, making a difference for other people actually makes you happier, and not only that, you live longer.

Interestingly, a recent study by nfpSynergy, a think tank and consultancy in the area of not-for-profit activity, entitled *The 21st Century Volunteer* has revealed a halt in the growth of volunteering, after several years of continuous growth, with some evidence of a small reversal of the trend. Their research reveals compelling reasons for this change in the trend.

The major reason they identify is that volunteers tend to be better educated, more discriminating, and more demanding. In all areas of their life they have huge choice as to how they allocate their scarce time resources. They are therefore demanding more time flexibility from charities, and more relevant and meaningful work. Currently, charities are very slow to respond with more intelligent and sensitive matching of needs to skills. A person skilled in information technology is still being handed a paintbrush, or a bin liner to collect litter.

Nowadays people want appropriate training, support and recognition, relevant work, and even a say in how operations are run.

Sadly, an effective delivery mechanism for matching an individual volunteer's potential contribution to needs is still some way off. The good news is that charities are beginning to appreciate the need, and the potential. The challenge is for charities to make their volunteer development and management as professional and effective as their fundraising development and management.

More important though, is that the whole perception of volunteering is changing. What previously was perceived as social obligation is now seen as a means for the individual volunteering to find self-fulfillment in helping others. The old Victorian paradigm of stern duty—the burden the wealthy middle classes must take up to help the less fortunate (poor) members of society—has been transformed. Volunteering is now about unleashing the personal potential of people at all levels in society. The benefits are now two-way—to the helper and the helped.

A powerful parallel of this mutual benefiting is my own experience in the London Marathon. I was lucky enough to run in the first four London Marathons. It was an uplifting and moving experience. Apart from the obvious discomfort and challenge of having to run such a very long way, the support of the crowd was energizing and moving to a degree impossible to communicate to someone who has not experienced it personally.

The route was lined by people cheering us on—often with wit, as well as encouragement (I remember one old lady, as our legs wilted towards the end, shouting "Don't worry dears, there's dancing at the end!"). The impact on the human spirit of all the runners was awesome. Time and again when the body and the mind were flagging, our courage and determination was restored by the cheers and encouragement of the crowd, many of whom had been standing there for two or three hours continuously cheering people on.

In subsequent years, my marathon career in suspension, I went with my family to support the runners. I was amazed to find it a very emotional and uplifting experience, almost more so than taking part. You felt that every runner you encouraged took strength from the exchange, and carried on fortified. The encouragement genuinely made a difference (as it had to me and my friends in earlier years).

The point is, as with volunteering, I was getting a big lift from helping others. In no way did I feel what was probably at the back of my mind when I first went to support those taking part—that I was doing the honorable thing in helping the runners, because I in turn had been helped. Rather than being noble, and repaying my dues, I found huge satisfaction and fulfillment in taking part in a reciprocal experience that benefited all parties. And it would have been just as fulfilling if I had never run a marathon in my life.

This fulfillment is manifest not just in a sense of spiritual fulfillment. Research amongst over 600 Community Service Volunteers (the organization is the UK's largest volunteering and training organization, with an interesting website, www.csv.org.uk) showed that there are direct physical and mental health benefits in volunteering. Not only is volunteers' mental health better, they take less sick days, and even enjoy noticeable weight loss. (Apart from the weight loss, this is remarkably similar to the positive health attributes mentioned earlier of optimists against pessimists.)

So the positive difference makers seem to be slowly building their numbers and their strength in our society. The next step is to explore how they can be helped to be more effective.

3

The elements of the mindset, and finding our purpose

Let's lay out the route to more effective difference making. Remember that the Make a Difference Mindset is the deliberate, conscious decision to make a positive difference: either to the people around us, or the situation in which we find ourselves. It is moving from what is now probably the somewhat random application of an unconscious competence at making a difference—something we do, without fully realizing how we do it—into a regular, consistent, conscious competence—something we are good at, because we have mastered the elements of improving lives and societies.

First of all we will examine our **Purpose**. We will take some time over this, as it is the wellspring of energy, determination, and delivery, and it can be quite challenging to pin down our specific purpose. However enormous the level of goodwill we may feel, without identifying the specific sources of this goodwill within our make-up, it can be quickly dissipated, and the benefits lost.

Within this we will plot our own **Values Map**, which will give us the biggest clues to exactly where we will focus our early activity in making a difference. Once we understand the true balance of our values, we can begin to build the **character, conscience, and courage** we will need to keep us strong on the journey.

We will then identify how we **add or create value** to make a difference, and we'll examine the type of difference we intend to make. We may want to tilt at windmills, in which case we'll become **Difference Drivers**. If we want to change things, but be part of a larger movement for change just starting, or already in progress, we'll become **Difference Deliverers**. And if we want to transform things for single individuals, or small numbers of people, we'll become **Beneficial Presences**.

We will examine the nature and priority of our goals. Which domains do they cover—work, sport, home, and so on—which are the most important, and which the most urgent, and which are both?

Finally we will look at how our purpose interacts with the **concept** we decide to focus our energies on, how we find our

stimulus to sustain our motivation, and how we **brand** our activity to make sure it is relevant, inspiring and instantly communicable.

FINDING OUR PURPOSE

This is the big one. If you can nail this one, all the other parts of the process make more sense and are more satisfying to apply. A meaningful pattern emerges. You have passion, and any stress is positive, energizing stress rather than negative, debilitating stress.

Crucially, finding our purpose makes it much easier to unlock the potential lying dormant within us (as my daughter said, the eyes to enhance the picture that still lie poised within our pencils). The writer John Buchan made the same point, "The task of leadership is not to put greatness into humanity but to elicit it, for the greatness is already there."

As you can guess, finding our purpose is not easy. A small minority of people have known their purpose since childhood, and have no need of guidance on the subject. For most of us, such a harmonization of mind and spirit is hard to achieve, and needs working on, even when it is achieved.

It is worth working on, though, because not only will it help you be more effective in making a difference, it may well help in other areas of your life. The job you have, or the allocation of the spare time you have, may change as a result of having a clear understanding of your purpose.

The first thing to say about clarifying our purpose is that if we can do it, we will be closer to understanding who we are as human beings.

So what is our purpose? What do we stand for? Which raises the question—who are we? *Who* we are, and *what we do*, are often two very separate things. Discovering our purpose will help us to understand better who we are.

This is a profound philosophical question, and not one we often ask ourselves. The very fact we feel we want to make a difference, however, sets us apart from other animals, which exist merely to eat, drink, and procreate. The desire to make a difference defines our humanity. We can envision not just the present, but also the future, and we want to leave the world a better place for our passing, and in better shape for those who follow us. This feeling is intensified by our growing understanding about the impact of our consumption habits on the planet, and the risks they pose to current, as well as future generations.

Such thoughts may not be uppermost in our minds, but they underpin our desire to be in some way accountable. If we are to be accountable, to what personal or wider moral framework are we accountable? What is important to us, and is that playing its rightful part in our lives?

Once we are more certain who we are, and what our purpose is, we can set about making decisions on where and how we are going to make a difference. The two are so closely linked, because purpose and service (making a difference) are cause and effect. How we add value to other people's lives is a direct manifestation of our purpose.

Discovering our purpose is not easy. We think we know ourselves, but when it gets down to it, most of us are pretty hazy on what exactly we stand for, and what our life priorities are.

Essentially, our purpose is our **reason for being**. If we don't have one at all, we drift helplessly. In the words of Goethe, "A life without purpose is an early death." It may be that loss of purpose is behind many of the world's major problems today. Depression—the major mental health challenge facing (particularly developed) societies around the globe—stems directly from it. Drugs, family breakdown, violence, lack of respect for people and institutions are supercharged by individuals having little connection to a positive purpose.

Discovering our purpose is, theoretically, simple. We need to ask ourselves the question, "What do I really love to do?" Because most of us haven't had an overwhelming desire since childhood to become an explorer or an artist, we don't have a ready answer.

So we have to probe. The next question is "What areas of my life do I get most satisfaction from?" In what situations do I get a special buzz? These buzzes can grow to something much bigger. Joseph Jaworski, in *Synchronicity: The Inner Path of Leadership* (a brilliant book) puts it this way:

> It is a call to service, giving our life over to something larger than ourselves, the call to become what we were meant to become—the call to achieve our vital design.

Our purpose may come to dominate our lives in this way, and if it does we are profoundly fortunate. But for most of us our vital design is a unifying theme for the different domains of our lives. If, for example, we were to discover our purpose is to use our creativity to make life better for the people around us, then this could manifest itself in several different ways, as we came to apply it to our different life domains.

In our work, we might transform a job that wasn't up till then benefiting from our full potential by applying our creative skills, and developing innovative ideas that improved the processes, products, or services of our organization. The job would become more enjoyable and satisfying, and more beneficial to our employers. Or if innovation of such a kind were not welcome, we could apply our creativity to humor, making colleagues laugh. Alternatively, we could think about creating charitable events, or involving our team in community work.

With our partner or family, we could decorate our home more inspirationally, or get involved in life-enhancing hobbies like painting, dance, or music. If we have no partner or family, we could develop a specific creative skill to a higher level—as a gardener, writer, or cook. In sport, we could innovate new coaching or training techniques, or in team games, devise new moves, develop new ways to improve team spirit.

You get the picture. In another brilliant book, Kevin Cashman's *Leadership from the Inside Out*, he defines the discovery of purpose, as "Purpose is the broad context that integrates all our life experiences. It is the defining thread that runs through and connects life's divergent experiences."

It is this **defining thread** we are looking for. Once we have found it, our vital design will crystallize. Cashman goes on, "Purpose is constant. The manifestation of purpose is always changing." This is important. How our purpose emerges, in terms of how we deliver it, can, and probably will, change as we go through life. So if our purpose in life is to help others learn, we may at one time work in human resources in an organization, at another as a teacher, and at another as the creator of teaching aids.

We may spend time helping adult immigrants, or their children, to learn our language better. At another time in our life, we may teach evening classes, or take on coaching roles in sport, or with disadvantaged children. All these activities are consonant with our purpose, and align the different domains of our life. They are linked by the defining thread of helping others to learn, but are very different as working experiences.

Once we have discovered our purpose, we can find meaning in our lives. All the bits start to work together. We are likely to find, however, that life is not tidy. There will be bits where duty is driving our behavior, rather than the energizing satisfaction of being on-purpose. Or other bits where conditioning has dulled our spirit into accepting things as they are, and it will be challenging to turn around to refresh them with meaning relevant to our vital design.

ACTUALLY NAILING OUR PURPOSE

So far we have the two questions:

"What do I really love to do?"
"What areas of my life do I get most satisfaction from?"

They are different questions, and both demand some time for reflection. I find it helpful to map things out on a piece of paper. If I don't, I find useful thoughts and half-thoughts slip away into the ether, never to return. If I jot them down on paper, I may have trouble deciphering them later, but at least I've caught most of them.

> The reason it is important to get them down on paper is that they are likely to be pretty random to start with. Unless you are blessed with a crystal-clear purpose, the message coming through will be wisps of feelings: a positive emotion, recalling an activity here, a glow of satisfaction at an achievement there, all building slowly into a pattern.

It may take several sessions of reflection to find that pattern. The defining thread may be slow to reveal itself. As other sources of inspiration and illumination, it may be worth trying the following:

- Carrying a notebook around with you, and jotting down the stimuli that make you feel worthwhile, uplifted, or fulfilled.
- Also jotting down what was happening or what you were doing when you felt energized and enthusiastic—who were you with, what was happening?
- Recalling what your dreams were as a child. What dreams do you have now? Cut out pictures from magazines and newspapers, and paste them into a dream book. Get the juices working on what excites you.
- Establishing the best time for meditation and reflection for you—on a run, listening to music, taking a shower, on a journey, and so on—and letting your subconscious have its say. Listen carefully to what it says—about your dreams, and the things you're trying to avoid—and make notes later.

> In a sense you are mapping your soul. There is an important spiritual element to understanding your purpose in life. Listening to the yearnings of your soul over time is key to the process of discovering that purpose. If it is slow to reveal itself, stick at it. It may take its time to yield up the treasure you are seeking, but yield it, it will.

4

The values map

You must be the change you want to make in the world.
Mahatma Gandhi

Getting to understand your purpose is, in a sense, solving the mystery of who you are. And the mystery is never quite solved. Uncertainty and ambiguity still lie around the edges, probably because doubt is part of the human condition.

Don't despair. Once we can identify the defining thread we will finally reach a point of stillness, which can be transformational. This point of stillness is reached when you finally get to the point when you just know that you have found the thing that makes you tick. You relax, because the things you enjoy doing, and the things you want to do, all flow from that pivotal, central point. Understanding this, as Gandhi intimates, is the necessary prerequisite for understanding the difference you want to make in the world.

A major aid to understanding purpose is to clarify our values. Values are part of purpose, and like purpose can be slippery and elusive. Some values are clear, some are less so, and some seem to change in importance over time. I revisit the relative importance of my values every couple of years or so, and I find interesting differences.

Looking at a values statement of some years ago, I see tidiness as a value that had some importance for me. The irreversible and glorious clutter of a growing family has meant it figures nowhere in more recent lists. Interestingly reward as a value has slipped from number eight some years ago to nowhere today. This surprised me at first, as whatever your income you usually spend out a bit more than comes in. It's still important, but no longer front of mind.

So how do we get a handle on our values? One of the most worthwhile thinkers and writers on values is Richard Barrett. Barrett was values coordinator at the World Bank (an interesting job in itself) and is an engineer by training, not a psychologist. This has enabled him to bring clarity and process to an area that can all too easily become either fuzzy, over-academic, or both.

Richard Barrett's book, *Liberating the Corporate Soul: Building a Visionary Organization* is a very good read, if you are interested in what is becoming recognized as one of the most important areas in business performance—the interface and harmony (or otherwise) between employees' personal values, and the values of the organizations they are employed by.

What Barrett does is to map the values of the employee, then map those of the organization, and then—the interesting bit—he gets the employee to map the values of the ideal organization to work for. He then explores the gaps between an employee's personal values, the values of the organization he or she would like to work for, and those of the organization itself. The gaps can be illuminating. Organizations are often surprised at the difference between what they believe their culture to be, its perception by their workforce, and how it should be developing it if they want to retain their best employees, and attract good new ones.

The reason I mention this is that for some readers, who are troubled by the dissonance between their values and those of the organization they are working for, it may be valuable to map the areas of dissonance. The mapping may help you to see if the challenges are serious enough to demand action. The action may be in terms of leaving and finding new employment, or deciding that a goal will be to stay, and make a difference to the values of the organization.

An example of this might be someone working in a care home for elderly people, where the management is more concerned with bureaucracy and profit than with service to old people. The choice would be either to leave, and find somewhere with more compassionate management, or to stay on and get the job satisfaction of helping the elderly, while making a difference by finding ways of convincing the management that it is in their interest to provide more humane service to their customers.

For the purposes of simplicity, in an area that isn't simple, we will be looking just at *personal values*, and trying to find a way to link them back to purpose that hopefully confirms, as well as illuminates, the work you have already done on discovering that purpose.

As we saw from Maslow's hierarchy, values break down into neat categories, beloved of the academics—physical, emotional, mental, spiritual, and so on. For the purpose of our Values Map we won't do this. The reason for this is that we want to get a picture of what is important to us, not what we think should be important to us. This avoids us looking at our list, and thinking, "I'm a bit light in the spiritual values category for someone who is intending to make a difference, so I'll bung a few more in, so it looks better."

Honesty in selecting our values is of paramount importance. We're doing this to help us finalize our purpose, so it's not about selecting values that make us feel good about ourselves. We need to start from a point of where we are now, not where we may arrive at later in our journey.

THE INGREDIENTS

The mapping—finding what direction we are headed in—comes later. First we need to look at the ingredients of our values set. The list below is an amalgam of values from various systems, plus one or two of my own that might be relevant. If there are values that you find important that aren't on the list, do add them. The map has to be personal and relevant to you.

The first step is to go down the list and circle the values that ring bells with you. You're looking for values that resonate, and are important to you.

If you don't want to mark the book, just get a photocopy of the page, and circle the relevant values on that.

Accountability
Ambition
Behaving morally
Being competitive
Being creative
Being liked
Belonging
Broad vision
Care for the environment
Caution
Community service
Control
Cooperation
Courage
Dialogue
Domain balance (physical, emotional, mental, spiritual)
Efficiency
Empathy
Enthusiasm
Fairness
Family
Flexibility
Focus
Forgiveness
Friends
Future generations
Kindness
Learning

Love
Gentleness
Harmony
Honesty
Humor/fun
Image—how others see you
Independence
Integrity
Knowledge
Meaning
Nutrition
Openness
Perseverance
Personal development
Physical exercise
Pride
Productivity
Respect
Responsibility
Reward
Security
Self discipline
Self improvement
Social responsibility
Status
Trust
Wealth
Wisdom
Work–life balance

THE MAP AND THE COMPASS

When you've circled the ones that that resonate with you, the interesting bit begins. You will now take the next step by ranking your values from 1 to 10. If you've less than 10, don't worry. If you've more than 10, leave the others there for the record, but they don't seem to be major motivators.

In deciding on the ranking, you are prioritizing what is important to you. You are deciding what presses your hot buttons. Thinking about it deeply, you may be surprised at the things that are very important to you, but are not getting their fair share of your attention and energies at the moment. These values are not aspirational ones, of the "this will make me feel good about myself" variety. They are "these are gut felt that I've been neglecting values."

You may find that one or two of these important values are too far away from where you are now to be honestly included in your current values ranking. Be very aware of them, and move towards them, but the current location of both purpose and action is your deeply held values as they are now.

Once you've got your top 10 values ranked, you can start to create your Values Map. Get hold of a piece of A5 card (post-card size), and place it in a portrait, rather than landscape, position in front of you. Use different colored pens to give each value more drama as you write it in. You can configure your values in any shape you wish on the card to make it more impactful and good to look at. Be imaginative, and have fun with it, creating a butterfly shape, a bird in flight, or whatever appeals to you.

There are only two stipulations to discipline your imagination. The first is that the values should be hierarchical. Your high-octane values should be towards the top of the card, and the slightly lower-octane of the 10 towards the bottom. The second is that your top two, three, or four leading values should be clustered into an arrowhead (which you can outline top center of your card, and will form part of your overall design) with your most important value at the top of the arrowhead, as close to the apex as you can fit it in.

The reason for this is that the arrowhead should give the overall design a sense of momentum. Looking at your Values Map you should feel a sense of progress towards your goal.

Your Values Map should become a working document you refer to regularly. It may take one or two attempts to make it feel right, and for it to look as attractive and welcoming as possible. Leave space, if you need it, for one or two of the important values that are gut-important, but are too far away from your current situation to include. Write them in a bright color, just below the arrowhead, but put them in brackets. Only remove the brackets when you have involved them in your life sufficiently for them to be there in their own right.

Maps are of little use without a compass to indicate what direction to travel in to find the place you are looking for. The values clustered at the top of the page in the arrowhead, towards which the whole map is moving, represent magnetic north.

Magnetic north moves over time, so no Arctic explorer can trust it. True north is unmoving, however, and the sure guide to find the North Pole. Our purpose, when we eventually define it, will be our true north, but our values represent our magnetic north. They may well change position on your map over time, and some may drop out to be replaced by others, but they are very helpful as a rough guide in finding our personal true north. Your top three or four values (positioned in the arrowhead) will give a good indication as to what is important to you in life, and where your purpose may lie.

The important thing to remember at this stage is that there are no *right* core values. Obviously if a core value were something like exploitation, that would be right off the Values Map for making a positive difference. But most of the other values are building up a picture of who you are, and are therefore neither right nor wrong. Some values may have to be encouraged, or further developed later, but for now honesty and accuracy is paramount.

Thinking profoundly about this, and then moving on to the next couple of activities, which also help you get close to your purpose and values, will begin to throw quite useful light on the core of that purpose. It will also highlight the important defining thread, as it weaves its way through your life's divergent experiences.

The next two steps, which conclude this section on discovering our purpose, are classics of the personal development books. As with much in those books, they can be pure gold. A friend of mine, Miles Protter, specializes in transforming companies by mapping the values of employees, and then exploring ways of aligning them with the purpose of those companies. He finds it works particularly well in areas such as safety. Using it, the rules and systems normally associated with such issues can be augmented by powerfully felt values. These values then become beliefs, which in turn become behaviors. The result is that the employees develop extreme safety awareness because safety resonates strongly with their core values, rather than because the rulebook says they have to do so.

In searching for employees' values, and where they find their individual meaning, he uses both these techniques. He says he sometimes finds hardened, macho hard hats reduced to tears by going through the exercises. So prepare to weep.

The obituaries

The first exercise is that of writing three short obituaries about yourself. You assume that you have recently passed away peacefully, and the obituaries make a fair summary of your life so far.

They are to be written first from the perspective of a child, real or imagined. The second is from the perspective of your wife, or partner, or nearest other. The third is from the viewpoint of a colleague where you work. If you don't work, write it from the point of view of someone you see on a regular basis.

This is a powerful way of making you take stock of your life to date. It interrupts the possibly goalless flow of your life. You are going through the motions, but are you achieving what you set out to achieve in the idealism of your youth? Are you the person you expected to be when you were young, and full of dreams?

Writing the obituaries will confirm the positive bits in your life—your significant achievements in being a good wife, husband, son, daughter, nephew, niece, friend, colleague, and so on. Or confirm the deeds you have done, and the accomplishments that are yours in whatever field or fields of sport, work, interests, and so on you have excelled in or been interested by.

Alfred Nobel's rethink

Alfred Nobel was born in 1833, in Stockholm, and was brought up in the cosmopolitan St Petersburg in a family of extremely successful and wealthy arms dealers. His father invented sea mines, used for the first time in the Crimea.

Alfred, like his father, made a difference. Sadly it was a negative difference. He invented dynamite, which was used first in the Franco–Prussian War of 1870. Much of his life was devoted to the development of weapons technology, and his global business contributed to the death and maiming of countless sons, husbands, fathers, and lovers around the world.

The story goes that his obituary, when it appeared in a national newspaper, was, with some justification, far from complimentary. It was particularly hurtful for both him and for his family because it appeared in error—he wasn't actually dead.

The shock was so great that it caused Nobel to rethink his life, and the legacy he wanted to leave. He later claimed that he had been interested in peace as a process throughout his life. He even defended himself by saying he had really developed dynamite for peaceful purposes. Indeed, he pioneered the theory of the possibility of mutual mass destruction obviating the need for war. He died in 1896, before the First World War knocked that theory on the head.

The point is that his reaction to the obituary jolted him so much that it triggered its apotheosis in the creation of the Nobel Peace Prize. Today Nobel is known globally as the man who helps peace to happen. His role in developing dynamite and other weapons of destruction is forgotten, and possibly forgiven.

Obituaries are always positive (the probing and exposures usually come later). So do look for the good, presenting yourself as someone who has achieved, but was cut off before the fruition of talents was complete. Be honest. If the fruition was far from complete, say so. The purpose of this exercise is both to confirm a promising start, but also to shock you. It provides a jolt, a stimulus to reassess your priorities, and to see if your life so far has been on-purpose.

The letter

The second, and for now last, exercise is to compose a letter. You write it to a young relative who has sought your advice, and asked you what you have found important and uplifting in your life. A key element is that the young person you are writing to is on your wavelength, and values similar things to you. The two of you connect very well. He or she will absolutely understand what you are writing about, and will greatly value your thoughts, wisdom, and lessons learnt.

The catch is that you are writing the letter imagining that you have reached the age of 75. If you are already 75 or more, just add 10 years to your current age. Your challenge is to create your life story for the intervening years. Having done so, you must define what you have achieved in the years between now and 75 (or beyond), as well as accounting for the achievements of your life to date.

The key to the letter is to be honest—and not over-modest—about your achievements. And to be open about your feelings towards them. It may be you feel one of your greatest achievements has been to retain your integrity under pressure from someone in authority. If that's the case, put it in the letter, and explain why the achievement is important to you.

What sort of achievements will you describe? Put in both what has made you proud in your life to date, and what you imagine you will achieve between now and your 75th birthday. What has made you feel most fulfilled? How will you find fulfillment between now and then? What lessons can you pass on from what you've learned?

Notice that this is a positive exercise. There is no place for regrets. No "might have beens" if things had turned out differently. This is about the sentiments of the ballad made famous by Frank Sinatra, "I did it my way." The letter should resonate with determination to be true to yourself, and pride in who that self is.

REPETITION AND PARADOXES

You may note some repetition between this exercise and the earlier exploratory work to explore purpose, and to perceive the defining thread linking the fulfilling parts of your life. This is entirely intentional. Coming at the exploratory process from more than one angle, and more important, allowing the element of repetition to tease out more of the truths which lie half-buried in your psyche, will enable more substantial progress to be made in getting a real handle on the still center of purpose.

Don't worry if paradoxes start to emerge. There are very likely to be contradictions in the different aspects of your life. Things won't seem to fit. The defining thread may at the present look more like loose ends that don't seem to come together.

This is not a five-minute job. As you get into it, and reflect deeply on the issues involved, a pattern will start to emerge. Think about it as you drift off to sleep. Think again when you wake up. Think about it in the odd cracks of time in your life. Doing the exercises requires some bravery on your part. Opening yourself up to this sort of examination needs courage and application. If you feel you're exposed during the process, it means you are getting out of your comfort zone, and exploring things that probably needed examining, but you were keeping hidden, even from yourself. If you do feel uncomfortable, make sure your writings, on paper or on computer, are well hidden from prying eyes. This is a personal voyage of discovery, not a team game.

Eventually the picture will come into focus, and you will experience a feeling of relief and release, as, at last, you know and understand your purpose.

5

The start point: being captains of our souls

Character, conscience, and courage

I took pleasure where it pleased me, and passed on. I forgot that every little action of the common day makes or unmakes character, and that therefore what one has done in the secret chamber has someday to cry aloud from the housetop. I ceased to be lord over myself. I was no longer captain of my soul.
Oscar Wilde, De Profundis

Making excuses is a whole lot easier than recognizing our own free will. Not everyone appreciates it, but we, and we alone, are responsible for our purpose, our values, our attitudes, our hopes, our enthusiasm, our self-confidence, and our courage. Some people, however, resist it, and cling to a deterministic comfort blanket, blaming their background, circumstances, or stress, for their actions and behaviors.

Recognizing our responsibility for our thoughts and actions is the first, and most major, step in getting in shape to make a difference. The next step is to acknowledge that this responsibility brings with it the need to behave with integrity across all domains in our life. The capacity to recognize responsibility and act consistently with conscience, resides in *character*.

Building our character means that we can, in Oscar Wilde's memorable phrase, become captains of our soul. Just as Abraham Maslow defined the choice between safety and growth as a daily event, so character is an ongoing choice.

Of course, you can make a difference without having a good character. I don't mean bad differences, like the ones Hitler made. I mean good differences made by people who pretend to want to be of service to others, because it helps their personal agenda. They can act the part of being Beneficial Presences, or a Difference Deliverer, but that is what it is—an act.

The interesting thing is that people can smell lack of integrity. Eventually, people who don't have it get found out. The great quote of Groucho Marx, "If you can fake sincerity, you've got it made," is funny, but ultimately not true. Faking sincerity is extremely difficult in the medium term, let alone the long term. Consistency is hard to sustain, cracks in the carefully constructed persona appear, and something foul-smelling begins to seep out. People get a whiff of this, and doubts begin to appear. Once doubts materialize, trust is compromised, and the person faking sincerity is found out very rapidly.

Character is about taking responsibility for who we are as well as what we do. Who we are precedes what we do. At its lowest level, it is about growing up.

Take the childish traits—blaming others ("it's not my fault"), petulance, loss of temper, ingratitude, refusal to listen, rudeness (lack of consideration for others), and arrogance. These need to be overcome, and transmuted into their opposites—being responsible for our failures, graciousness, and so on. This is what growing up is about, and it is what building character is about.

I touched earlier on the difference between character and persona. Character is about what goes on inside—integrity, trustworthiness, courage, perseverance, compassion, inclusion, and so on. Persona is what happens on the outside, our coping mechanisms to deal with life on a daily basis, our image, personality—our doing, rather than our being.

As we all know, sometimes tough decisions have to be made, because they are the right decisions. These decisions tend to be made from character. Persona tends for look for popularity, and popularity is an uncertain guide for good decision making.

Both character and persona are important, but the first is a lot more important than the second. Character underpins persona. Unless it is based on strong character, persona is vulnerable. It breaks down under pressure, and is extremely hard to rebuild. With strong character, persona can still break down under pressure, but can be rapidly and strongly rebuilt.

SO HOW DO WE BUILD CHARACTER?

If we're serious about wanting to make a difference, we have to work on character, to make sure we are the best we can be. In fact, working on character is both motivating and rewarding. We can build our self-respect, and with it, our knowledge that we are a worthwhile human being.

Remember Wilde's statement: "Every little action of the common day makes or unmakes character."

The steps we need to take to become captains of our souls are as follows:

1. Take full responsibility

For everything. Your purpose, attitudes, behavior, energy, and your actions. No weaseling out. Don't expect anyone else to do it for you. Any blame for shortcomings is yours, and yours alone. Things that life throws at you can seem unfair, and probably are. Forget feeling sorry for yourself. You are in charge of your response to it. You are responsible for your health, happiness, and your fulfillment. If you're committed to making a difference, you're committed. You are not a victim of anything.

Mind the gap

This slogan from the London Underground has for over a century warned travelers to beware of the gap between the platform and the train. A key part of taking responsibility is rewriting your internal scripts. You are not the victim of either your conditions, or your conditioning. Stephen Covey—one of the great writers on personal development—identifies one of the fundamental steps in rewriting your internal scripts as coming to understand the opportunities presented by what he calls the gap between stimulus and response.

This gap is the split second—and it can be almost instantaneous until we learn to control our temper—between something happening, and our reaction to it. For instance, if you have been conditioned to assert yourself strongly if someone makes jokes at your expense about your race, sexual orientation, religious belief, or even the football team you support, you immediately feel the anger rising as this happens. Instead of letting the anger continue to rise, with the inevitable consequences—control it.

This intercession between the stimulus and response can be extremely challenging. I don't underestimate it in any way. If you feel part of a downtrodden minority, and you have pride in who and what you are, the temptation to stand up for yourself is immense. The trouble is in reacting—giving the response the person winding you up is looking for—you are handing power to them. As soon as you give them the prize they seek—your hurt and anger—they have won. It is like saying to them, "You don't like who or what I am. Here's a stick to beat me with."

Learning to take advantage of this gap between stimulus and response is crucial to growing up. It is moving from being a child, who reacts spontaneously to any stimulus, with no regard for, or understanding of, the consequences, to being an adult, who has learned to control this short-fuse response to the triggers to action lying in wait around us. Every time you feel the internal scripts, with their programmed response, arising within you, take a deep breath. You can overcome your conditioned response. Remember, mind the gap—falling into it can be uncomfortable and dangerous.

The good news is that it won't be long before you start not only mastering the gap, by controlling your responses, but also feeling good about yourself for doing so. As you progress, your ongoing choices will validate your character, and confirm your self-esteem and dignity. I'm not talking about dignity in the shallow persona sense. I'm talking about dignity in the sense of centered, well-founded self-esteem.

If you're starting from a pretty low base, don't worry. We all have to start somewhere. Just take very small steps to start with. Control negative responses (like blaming others for something that is clearly your responsibility) just once a day—or even once a week, if that is too difficult. Then, over time, move onto bigger steps, like controlling your temper most of the time. As you progress, you'll be able to make the really big steps, like keeping your word all of the time.

Importantly, for people concerned with making a difference, as you take more responsibility for yourself, you will find an appetite develops to take responsibility for others. You will find a significant shift taking place. While previously you felt you *ought* to make a difference, more and more you will find that you *want* to make a difference.

---

2. Practice being yourself in all situations

If we are caring and responsive people who believe we should be making a difference to help others, the chances are we sometimes find ourselves bending who we really are to accommodate what we feel others think we are, or would like us to be. We are back again to Maslow's daily 1000 choices between safety and risk.

We need to take risks to confirm our integrity, in order to resist the temptation to be the appropriate person to fit the environment. We all tend to be slightly different people in different situations. Indeed, psychologists have identified that we have a dominant personality, which is supplemented by up to 150 subpersonalities. These subpersonalities are fine and normal when the role demands it—the role you play as a son or daughter, for example, is different from the role you play as a father or mother. Even in these roles, the essential you should remain unchanged.

This is important, because the challenge comes when this accommodation of the role or the situation goes too far, and the dominant personality is compromised. This is the point when you find yourself in the situation of almost manipulating your persona to fit a tricky situation. When you find yourself doing this, you know you have gone well beyond what is wise or acceptable. You must quickly get back to who you are, and stay there.

As a daily exercise in the early days of character development, when such situations occur, it is worth asking yourself the question, "Am I acting from character, or from persona?" Determine to move day by day towards making character primary, and persona secondary.

This does not mean hurting others by making a brutal statement of the new you. If, for example, you find yourself in a situation where the people around you are accommodating, and participating in, a situation that is morally offensive—fiddling their expenses, or stealing from their employers—the situation needs to be dealt with strongly, but sensitively.

To say the whole thing is dishonest, and they are crooks, may be true, but is probably not the best way to proceed. Some of the people involved may be good people, and do what they're doing through accepting an amoral culture they feel they have no power to change. A more effective way might be for you to be strong, resist the cultural pull, stating quietly that you personally are not comfortable with the accepted practices, and are declining to partake in them.

By being strong—and being yourself—but not being directly offensive to your colleagues, you may find that some join you in stopping the shabby behavior. As a result, you can make a real difference by making a significant improvement to the environment and culture. The other basically honest colleagues will feel relieved at the change. Importantly, for them, the stress they are probably feeling at having to act out of character will be greatly reduced.

By being ourselves in all situations, we too will feel a reduction in our level of stress. Research confirms that one of the major sources of stress is the conflict of values between the different areas of our lives, the most common being work and home.

Why does this stress occur? The answer is simple. Because we only have one subconscious. We cannot kid our subconscious that we are this person for part of the day, and someone else for the rest. The subconscious of a healthy human being cannot be schizophrenic. Our subconscious has one identity for us—it has a fundamental integrity—so experiences dis-ease when faced with attempting to be a different character, according to the time of day.

If we define a clear and consistent ethical base for our activity across the entirety of work, family and social contribution, a weight can be lifted from us. That potentially enervating stress of conflicting values between our work and other aspects of our lives is resolved.

Our deeply held values are validated, and our behavior can once more become spontaneous and natural.

Remember, it is nice to be liked and respected. But it is more important to like and respect yourself. The validation of your authentic self comes from you, and you alone.

3. Listen to your conscience (not just because you should, but also because it may reveal your purpose)

Conscience is the litmus test for integrity. It tells us what is right and what is wrong with unfailing accuracy. It is through listening to, and acting in accordance with, our conscience that we become captains of our souls.

Conscience is the internal manifestation of the framework of unalterable principles that should guide our lives. Like the subconscious, it is a widely validated phenomenon over time, place, and culture. It embodies our sense of good and evil, right and wrong. It is the inner voice that is magically independent from upbringing and social context. Immanuel Kant called it "the moral law within."

It is particularly important to people wanting to make a difference, for two reasons. First, because the fundamental principles it reflects—not hurting others, or benefiting from their discomfort—are the source, if deeply felt, of compassion. It is compassion that drives our desire to make a difference.

The second reason is even more profound. In listening to our conscience, and responding with compassion, we sometimes discover both our purpose and a vehicle to fulfill that purpose.

It can take time to reveal and confirm itself, but little by little, as we respond to our conscience, we build and clarify our purpose. If that clarification centers on a specific activity, like helping a vulnerable group in society who are being exploited, or teaching IT skills to the under-qualified unemployed, this may over time become a specific project, and ultimately a movement. Many great charities, and great movements, have started in this way.

The extraordinary thing about conscience is that it transcends the values by which we were brought up. If we were brought up in a racist family, or were strongly influenced by a sexist father, we can, if we take the time to listen to our inner voice, feel that those values are wrong. When people listen to their conscience, timeless principles take over.

A story that reflects the powerful role conscience can play in our lives in guiding the actions that stem from character comes from Stephen Covey, when he was talking to an audience of bright, but somewhat cynical, young undergraduates. There were about 150 students there, in cramped, almost threatening conditions. The subject chosen was "The new morality"— which was shorthand for morality being a changeable feast, dictated by circumstances.

The so-called situational ethic means that there are no absolute morals or standards. Every situation is different, and has to be looked at in terms of the people involved, or other factors present. Covey flatly repudiated the proposition, going on to propose that there are a set of unchanging principles that underpin our lives.

There were two students in the front row who were particularly clever and articulate, and kept refuting Covey's points with skill and aggression. Covey felt surrounded and alone. Finally, in near-desperation, he held up his hand, and asked for silence. He then said, "Each of us knows the truth of these matters in their heart." He then asked each student there to think—in total silence—for a full minute, and to ask their heart the question, "Is the subject (The new morality), as it is explained here, a true principle, or is it not?"

He then said that if at the end of the minute they still believed it to be true, they could dismiss him, and he would leave. As the minute ticked slowly away, Covey looked out over the bowed heads, and sensed a change of mood in the meeting. At the end of the minute, he spoke to the most difficult and persuasive student, and asked, "In all honesty, my friend, what do you hear?"

After a pause, the student replied, "What I heard was not what I have been saying." Covey went on to continue his talk, and found the students had become less intellectual and defensive, and more open and teachable.

Acknowledging the existence of conscience, and listening to its promptings, is one thing. Obeying them consistently is quite another. It is all too easy to go with the enticements of the situational ethic. We adapt to the situation to meet our personal goals, and before you know it, our key achievement becomes not doing the right thing, but not getting caught. Manipulation and sly ducking and diving become core skills, and the chances of building character are destroyed utterly.

WHAT EXACTLY IS CONSCIENCE?

Conscience is a pretty elusive thing to define, but a useful definition is to think of it in these terms:

Conscience is the feeling in your gut that tells you:

- What is kind, and what is unkind
- What is fair, and what is unfair
- What is right, and what is wrong
- What is just, and what is unjust
- What is helpful, and what is hurtful
- What is selfless, and what is selfish
- What is loving, and what is unloving
- What is true, and what is false
- What is caring, and what is uncaring.

In essence, conscience perceives life as part of the total human existence—that is, what makes society, the environment we exist in, our ecology, work better. It's centered on integrity, service, and love—because it recognizes the importance of others. It puts our feelings and desires in the context of a more important whole.

Listening to our consciences, we know when we are not speaking the truth. This deep instinctive knowledge of the truth can be uncomfortable. If you work for an oil company that claims carbon emissions have no impact on global warming, and global warming isn't happening anyway, and then you sit down and listen to your conscience, you'd be pretty likely to end up, like Covey's student, saying "What I've heard is not what I have been saying."

This doesn't just apply to oil company employees. It applies to most of us at some time in our lives when we suppress conscience, and refuse to listen to it. We can get pretty good at it. But if we are serious about making a difference in the long term, we must be open to our conscience, listen to it, and act in accordance with what it tells us.

Conscience is the thing that keeps us on the straight and narrow. Its insistent, and sometimes uncomfortable, promptings give us a clear guide as to how to behave and what to do. If we listen to it, and heed its promptings, building our integrity day by day, we will indeed become captains of our souls, and learn to become consistently good at making a difference.

4. Courage

Courage is a basic prerequisite for our quest to make a difference. By definition making things different means changing those things from what they were to a new state. To accomplish this we are pretty certain to encounter forces that have a vested interest in keeping things the way they were. These forces (and inertia is one of the most powerful of them) are unlikely to cede the benefits of the status quo without a fight.

So sooner or later we are going to need courage to take on these forces, and make things happen. Let's look at courage and examine its nature, which is not altogether as obvious as it might appear at first sight.

The interesting thing about courage is that it is subjective and relative, not objective and absolute. By this I mean it is not the objective act that matters, and what at first sight looks amazingly courageous is sometimes not courageous at all. The reality is that it is the degree of challenge that the act poses to the individual at that time, and in those specific circumstances, that counts. It is not the act per se which allows us to assess how courageous an act it is.

Downhill ski racers will certainly need courage when pushing to the limits when they are in a competition. But when skiing recreationally, swooping down the mountain at a leisurely pace for fun, they will still be traveling at a velocity which would terrify the rest of us, but they will be so far within their capabilities they will require virtually no courage at all. A walk to the shopping center would be totally unchallenging to most of us, but for a frail elderly person, in fear of being mugged for his or her pension, it could be an act of huge courage. For someone who is profoundly depressed, just getting out of bed can be an act of great courage.

Courage—physical, moral, or intellectual—is the direct correlation between the amount of fear we feel, and the amount of strength of character we have to summon up to overcome it. We all feel fear at one time or another. It is entirely natural and healthy, in that it can protect us from danger.

So why specifically is courage so necessary for people wanting to make a difference? There are several reasons, and these are the most important of them. We need courage to:

- **Get out of our comfort zones.** As identified earlier, the great enemy of change is inertia. We sit in our comfort zones and it's all too easy to find making a difference inconvenient. It is Maslow's 1000 choices a day between comfort and growth—we settle for comfort, lacking the courage to take the risks involved in growth. Getting out of our comfort zones involves things we would rather not do— like talking to people, and trying to convince them of the need for change. It may also involve changing our own thinking. If we are trying to change the songbook, it may be that we need to compose some new tunes.

- **To develop our character through every action of the common day.** Character builds courage, but courage is needed to build character. It sounds like chicken and egg, but in fact both need each other, and feed off each other. As I said, building character is essentially about growing up. To move from being frozen in a childish state to adulthood takes courage, because the behaviors of infants remain with us as a comfort blanket of easy solutions to life's challenges. It's not our fault. Someone else—not us—is responsible for things going wrong, or life not being a bed of roses. Courage is needed all through the day to resist the easy option of blaming others, and to start taking the actions of mature adults to improve both our attitudes and our behavior.

- **To mind the gap.** This is an integral, but easily forgotten, part of the point above. We can be concentrating on the wider issues of building our character—taking responsibility, behaving honorably, not being selfish, and so on—and can be caught out by our spontaneous responses to life's challenges. The words of anger or blame have escaped our lips before we've had time to think, undoing much of the good work we may have accomplished during the day. We need courage to freeze our conditioned responses to given stimuli, which often involve giving up power to others who seek such responses. Minding the gap gives us time to consider our reactions, take back control, and behave with maturity and dignity.

- **Stand for something.** Standing for something involves risks. Going against the flow of popular opinion to effect change is unlikely in the short term to win any popularity contests. We need courage to be true to ourselves, and our cause. Things will only be made different if we are steadfast in our beliefs and our actions.

We may have honor, dignity, and self-respect, but we can't just have them in private. We will frequently have to assert them in public, and under adverse conditions.

- **To be responsible for our hope, enthusiasm, self-confidence, and energy.** Comfort and security are not natural states. When they exist, it is normally for short periods. Once we accept this, we know we are on our own, and how we feel and cope is in our own hands. We have freedom of will, and choice, and the unavoidable companion to freedom of any sort is responsibility. We have freedom to choose who we are, what we do, and what we will become. We need courage to take responsibility for those choices.

- **To cope with rejection.** Taking risks to improve things for the better—to make difference—inevitably increases the risk of rejection. People will stand in our way—and will be brutally frank about what they think of us and our efforts. When you are doing your best to improve things, it somehow seems doubly unjust to be told that you, and your efforts, are worthless. This is especially so if the resistance is delivered in a way that is aggressive or even venomous, as is often the case with people trying to protect their territory, or the status quo. Rejection is part of the stock in trade of Difference Drivers and Difference Deliverers. So courage has to be too.

- **To cope with failure.** To fail is to be human. If the differences we aim to make are substantial, they will be challenging to achieve, and will inevitably involve failure at some point. Failure, as they say, is the breakfast of champions. Sometimes overwhelming at the time, in hindsight it is the source of great learning. The acronym FAIL—First Action In Learning—is worth remembering. It can be profoundly annoying, but the truth is that we learn more from our failures than our successes. For difference makers, the feeling of defeat can be more than annoying. Because we are striving to make things better, we feel we have moral right on our side, so the emotional involvement is deeper, and the disappointment greater.

We cannot avoid the sometimes gut-wrenching disappointment, so we need courage to recover faster, and learn our lessons. In the words of Albert Camus, the French existentialist writer, "What does not kill me, strengthens me."

- **To hang in for the long term.** Some differences don't happen overnight. If you are a Beneficial Presence nursing someone with an incurable disease, the difficulty of the situation is relentless, the pressure unabated. We need courage to press on, through the long days and nights. If we are Difference Deliverers, pushing for society to change its behavior, again we are in for the long haul. We need courage to hang on in there, despite the difficulties. On a more down-to-earth level, courage can manifest itself as doggedness under pressure. Our elder daughter Tansy exhibited this at school when studying for her A Levels—the exam that would qualify her for university. In Art, her teachers were heavily resistant to her painting pictures on very large canvases. Under great pressure, she continued to make, and paint, large canvases (some much bigger than a large door). She was lucky enough to earn 99 percent in her exam, and it was with some satisfaction she found she had made a small difference to the thinking of teachers when she saw in a later edition of her school magazine a boast by the art department on the success their pupils were having with large canvases.

- **To take action.** Actually doing something is fundamental to making a difference. Once more, by definition some action needs to be taken in order for things to be made different. Procrastination all too easily sets in, and we defer action until a later day, when it won't be so inconvenient. Defining what needs to be done, what difference should be made, is sometimes relatively easy. Making it happen is quite another matter. In the words of the great management expert Peter Drucker, "Every great idea eventually degenerates into hard work."

- **To serve.** The capacity to serve—the essence of most difference making—is a mature and courageous response to the situation we find ourselves in. It takes guts to decide to not take the easy way out. Not to keep our heads down, and let the unacceptable status quo remain unchanged. The courage to be generous and selfless—to put the needs of others above those of yourself—is what defines Difference Drivers, Difference Deliverers, and, of course Beneficial Presences.

A LITTLE EXTRA HELP

This chapter is about character and some of the fundamental elements of our make-up, so it is with some trepidation that I am going to describe an NLP (neuro-linguistic programming) technique to shore up courage. It would be dismissed by the heavyweight personal development teachers as a sticking plaster solution, and unworthy of mention.

I am of the belief that sticking plasters can be very useful things, and are sometimes vital in the protection of wounds that might otherwise not get better without them. The truth is that when you're scared, you're scared. However much courage you have, you could always do with a bit more. The fundamental principles of character and courage apply of course, but a little help never goes amiss.

The technique is what I call becoming a Mighty Lion. If we are in a state of fear it can be very handy to have a method of reducing or even eliminating that fear.

The theory is that we have enabling states, and paralyzing states. Enabling states are states in which we feel joy, confidence, love, inner strength, ecstasy. Paralyzing states are states in which we feel anxiety, confusion, depression, low self-worth, sadness, and of course fear. Our behavior tends to be a direct result of the state we are in. In order to have courage, and to make a difference, we of course need to be in an enabled state. It is helpful at times to be able to summon up this state at will.

To develop this ability, you start by creating what is called an anchor. An anchor is a sensory stimulus linked to a specific state—similar to the bell that started Pavlov's dogs salivating, once they had been conditioned to believe they were about to receive food. (The Russian physiologist had programmed them to expect food at every ring of the bell, and when the food was removed, they still salivated in anticipation of the non-existent food.)

To create the anchor, you select a physical gesture—say, crooking your index finger—and then preconstruct a whole battery of positive feelings associated with it. To do this, you select four or five experiences in your life when you felt empowered to a very high degree. This could be taking part in a big sporting event, playing a solo part in a public concert, being applauded for a speech, being honored for an achievement at a business conference, or just being deeply thanked for an act of kindness you had done for somebody.

Whatever the events you select, it is important to relive them in all the color, sound, smells, and emotion of the event itself. While you are programming the anchor (do it 5 to 10 times) it is helpful to sit up, or stand up, with the chest out, so the body mirrors the pride you are feeling at reliving your moments of triumph. Once you have programmed them into the selected anchor—the crooking of the index finger, or whatever gesture you select—you can then start to mine the benefits.

When you're feeling low, or in a paralyzed state, just make the selected gesture, and experience the feeling of confidence and empowerment sweep through you. I still find his a very useful technique for tricky situations, although my first experience with it was somewhat ambivalent. I had, foolishly as it turned out, used the pressure of my thumb onto my forefinger as my anchor. A couple of days later, I went for a run, and towards the end, found I had overdone it somewhat, and decided to ease off a bit over the last kilometer.

To my surprise, rather than slowing down, I found myself running faster and faster, right to the end. It was sometime later, and after I was considerably out of breath, that I discovered the cause of this extraordinary phenomenon. Without realizing it, during the discomfort that had caused me to decide to slow down, I had started to clench my fist, and had activated my Mighty Lion anchor. The result was that I started running faster, rather than slower. The anchor had given me an entirely unintentional storming finish to my run—one that I took some time to recover from.

To return to the more permanent and fundamental aspects of the subject of this chapter, David Schwartz, in his magnificent book, *The Magic of Thinking Big*, talks about the temptations of inaction. His remedy is the following terse injunction: "If the spirit doesn't move you, sit down and move your spirit." The capacity to do this derives from character, and that important ingredient within character, courage.

Character and courage move us from depression to purposeful action. They move us from boredom to enthusiasm, and from passive to active. However strong and clear our purpose is, there are times when we need the concentrated strength of positive will from our character. It drives our attitudes, which in turn drive our behaviors. It produces the service to others over and above the expected, the going of the extra mile that makes the difference.

The really difficult bit is that building character and courage is in our own hands. We may accept this intellectually as a concept, but we tend to fight it tooth and nail emotionally. Taking the significant step to engage in this process emotionally is how we become captains of our souls. And it is a major step in preparing ourselves to be consistently good at making a difference.

6

Now we know why, we move on to how: creating value for others

We now approach the heart of the matter—the reason for this book's existence.

Finding our purpose seeks to define *why* we want to help our fellow humans. The next stage is to define *how* that help—that difference we want to make—will emerge. We will then move on to a coherent *method* to make that delivery effective.

In essence, serving our fellow human beings—making things better for them (which is what making a difference is about)—is about creating value for them. Value is an interesting word. We all think we know what it means, but interpretations can differ widely. The most frequent use of the word is in commerce, where the word is screamed from posters claiming the best value in town. Because of this usage, one meaning of the word has come to be low-priced, even cheap.

In fact, value in commerce is an equation. It is an article's relationship between its quality and its price. So very expensive things, like a palace or a Ferrari, can be good value, as long as their quality and the benefits they provide are high in relation to their price. It is an extremely useful word, because mainstream meanings ("I really value your help," "It's valuable to me") are free of the low-price connotations, and convey a strong sense of an object, or action, being of benefit, or worth.

It is the latter meaning that is relevant to making a difference. To make a difference to a person or a situation, we need to create value. This may be new value, or just the provision of an existing benefit. The value can be financial, but it is more likely to be psychological, physical, or even spiritual. Creation of new value can be as simple as the invention of wheels on a suitcase. This has provided massive benefit to countless people, making a huge difference in reducing the load people have to carry when traveling.

ADDING OR TAKING VALUE: IT'S THE INTENTION THAT COUNTS

In our daily lives we all create or add value, and we also take value. Taking value can be negative and destructive, or it can be positive and enhancing. An example of the negative taking of value is elements within the global financial system. Although the system overall provides massive benefit in enabling business to function efficiently and effectively, large parts of processes involved in the system create no value. While creating no value, they still reward the financiers, bankers, stockbrokers, and lawyers hugely for their efforts.

Many of the processes—dealing, trading on exchange rates, and so on—seem not only to add no value, but also to take huge sums of money out of the system for the sole benefit of the banks and financial institutions making the gambles. The individual traders receive obscene sums of money for removing other people's money from the system.

Interestingly, many of the workers earning huge incomes from such activities suffer from high levels of stress. This stress is, of course, partly to do with the pressure and intensity of their daily tasks.

An important part of the stress, which often causes burnout, however, seems to stem from the worthlessness of the activities they are undertaking. They are not just adding no value in what they do all day, they are taking out huge financial value.

To exaggerate the situation, they are being paid huge sums for stealing money from other people. However honorable they may be as individuals, their subconscious knows what is going on. You can't fool your subconscious. If your subconscious believes you are taking value, and giving nothing in return, it will be sending messages to your conscience to say that something is wrong.

Taking value is not always wrong. If we work for an organization that trains us, then we are taking value from that organization. What is important here is the intention. If we are benefiting from the training so that we can do a better job for our organization, then that is a win/win for both parties. If we are hanging on in a job just to get the training, in order to go elsewhere and get a higher-paid job, then that is taking value, and is a form of theft.

Graciousness when receiving value can be a way of adding value. When someone praises us for something we have done for them and we don't accept the praise graciously we are, in a sense, taking value from them. If we affect modesty, mumble and change the subject, we are depriving them of a proper response to their praise. It is tantamount to rejecting it. We have taken and wasted the value they have created by articulating their gratitude to us for our efforts.

ADDING VALUE THROUGH MAKING PEOPLE FEEL VALUED

This is possibly the most immediately impactful value any of us can create. Countless studies have shown that stress and anxiety, especially amongst the socially disadvantaged, is brought about through not feeling valued—by other individuals, or by society.

In the socially deprived, this feeling at its most extreme is articulated as a strong reaction to being "dissed"—shown disrespect by others, which often leads to violence. Over 200 studies in this area alone have shown that threats to self-esteem and social status are the biggest producers of the stress that leads to violence.

So genuinely making others feel valued is potentially a huge contribution to human happiness. The most direct way to do this is to offer people friendship. Friendship reduces stress, because it involves people socially. It is based on reciprocity, mutuality, social obligation, and the recognition of others' needs.

Friendship, like an optimistic outlook, also protects against illness. A medical study where cold virus nose drops were introduced to a very large sample of volunteers showed that those with friends were four times less likely to develop a cold than those without friends.

Providing friendship is the core role of Beneficial Presences. In doing this, they not only support others, often in times of need, they make them feel valued through that support, and in so doing reduce stress, and improve their physical and mental health.

ADDING AND TAKING VALUE IN FAMILIES

In families, the balance between adding value and taking value varies over time. For example, however much some parents give, their children want to take more. Other children give back more than they take. Often this value lies in the people they become as they grow up and become adults. Seeing children realize at least part of their potential is hugely rewarding for parents, and creates huge value for them, and for all concerned.

The creation of value within a family has many manifestations, but the most basic, and the most fundamental, is the creation of a sense of security for children growing up. This is not financial security—no one can guarantee that—but personal security based mainly on a sense of justice.

Justice and fairness are often core values in making a difference. Whether we are saving the planet or teaching a class of children, justice and fairness underpin our attitudes and our behaviors, and in themselves create value. Establishing clearly what the rules and the boundaries are—with consistent enforcement of those rules and boundaries (and with consistent penalties for breaking them)—creates a sense of security. Families, like societies, gain their stability through a framework of fair rules, fairly enforced.

The lack of a clear ethical framework means rules can be bent or broken. Within a family, if there is no consistency, there is no integrity. Children grow up learning that being manipulative brings more benefits than being good. In the short term, they may feel they are winners, but in the long term they are major losers, and their families have failed them.

Another source of security within a family—for both children and adults—comes from unconditional love. Unconditional love creates huge value by confirming a child's sense of intrinsic worth. An important way to create value is to make people feel valued. However high our self-esteem is, most of us still benefit from a sense that we are valued by others. It confirms and validates us as individuals. Unconditional love is the highest form of being valued.

By the same token, there is no more effective way of taking value from someone—especially a child—than withdrawing unconditional love. Indeed, a significant elephant trap in family relationships is the temptation to step back from unconditional love for certain family members. This temptation is exacerbated by the potential complexity and complicatedness of what now constitutes a family.

Second and third marriages bring with them step-children who don't always get on. Not only do they not get on, some of them are full of anger because they are emotionally damaged. This anger can be directed at parents, or step-parents.

The anger is deeply felt, and can be extremely hurtful for the recipients of the anger and abuse. Whether they are parents or step-parents, it is difficult for them to keep it in mind that the anger is not really directed at them personally, but is the eruption of hurt caused by other problems. For parents or step-parents to respond with unconditional love is extremely challenging. For them, it seems like value is being taken from them on a daily, even hourly, basis, and the pain of that loss of value is keenly and damagingly felt.

But once love is seen as partial and discriminatory by the hurt young family member, trust begins to break down. The possibility of creating value for the young person (so much in need of it) is severely reduced, and temporarily at least, lost completely. The only long-term solution is the return to unconditional love. This can be very difficult, but ultimately it is one of the highest forms of value creation for others, and one of the most effective ways of really making a difference.

In practical terms, the only solution may be to concentrate on being a Beneficial Presence for that person. This may be met with consistent and violent rejection while the hurt is still raw. This is why the building of character and courage is important for difference makers. Being a Beneficial Presence may sound like a soft option—all you have to do is to be there, and smile benignly. But when the going gets tough—and dealing with visceral family situations can be very tough—guts and resilience are required as well as kindness and love.

TAKING AND CREATING VALUE FOR THE PLANET

The creation of value is fundamental to making a difference, but we must recognize before we go further that not all differences that need to be made require its creation in the short term—although longer-term the creation of value can be immense.

Let's look at the story of Bob Hunter. Back in the early 1970s Hunter was an iconoclastic journalist on the *Vancouver Sun.* Vancouver was his adopted city, but he had grown to love it and its people. He started attending meetings in the basement of a church. The subject of the meetings was how to put pressure on Canada's neighbor, the United States, to stop its program of nuclear testing in the Aleutian Islands, off Alaska. He christened the group the "Don't Make a Wave Committee"—alluding to the massive waves created by nuclear tests.

The group agreed that the best way to protest against the tests was in the location they were taking place. As a result, Hunter and a few like-minded friends rented a rusting fishing vessel called the *Phyllis Cormack*, and set sail for Amchitka Island, where the next test was due to take place. He thought he was just going to be the reporter taking notes, and indeed he sent some hilarious dispatches on the 45-day voyage back to the *Vancouver Sun*.

He ended up on watch, however—involved in the running of the ship—as well as sending back his reports. It was his reports on their presence in the area and the reasons for it, which began to create paralyzed indecision in Washington. President Richard Nixon came under severe pressure and eventually announced the abandonment of the series of tests, declaring Amchitka Island a wildlife refuge, which it remains to this day.

Before they had set sail, they had renamed the boat *Greenpeace*. From that early initiative came the environmental organization, which today has over 2.5 million members in over 40 countries. Even more extraordinary is that Greenpeace is now one of the largest global brands in terms of awareness, and the highest rated in terms of trust.

Hunter became its first president, and when he died in 2005 he received glowing tributes from around the world. Gerd Leipold, executive director of Greenpeace, said of him:

> Bob was a storyteller, a shaman, a word-magician, a Machiavellian mystic, and he dared to inject a sense of humor into the often shrill and sanctimonious job of changing the world. He was funny and brave and audacious, inspiring in his refusal to accept the limits of the practical or the probable. He reveled in life's ability to deliver little miracles in the form of impossibilities achieved, and Greenpeace will forever bear the mark of his crazy, super-optimistic faith in the wisdom of tilting at windmills.

This quote in fact came to hand after I had written the earlier chapters of this book, but it echoes them uncannily. Another commentator said of him, "This was a man with a great loving heart, a brilliant mind, and a massive spirit."

Hunter made a difference by *preventing* things happening. Indeed most people fighting for improvements in ecological and environmental behavior are trying to prevent the depredations caused by the greed of corporations, governments, and humankind in general. The point of the Greenpeace story, however, is that Hunter, one of the key Difference Drivers, and who evolved into a Difference Deliverer, had the objective of creating value for the world—in all its various animal, vegetable, and mineral forms. He did this by preventing abuse by the powerful. But the whales, dolphins, and other fauna and flora still alive today, which wouldn't be otherwise, attest to the value he created.

CREATING VALUE THROUGH LEADERSHIP

The essence of leadership is adding value to people. It is the ability to give a team, an organization, or a movement, a vision that resonates with their emotions and with their souls. It is about making the people that follow feel inspired that they are working for a worthwhile purpose or cause. It is the ability to give meaning to what they are doing.

There is a simple story that illustrates the potential to give energy and direction to people by creating a bigger picture, which gives meaning to the day-to-day tasks they are performing. The story goes that there was a row of stonemasons chipping away at blocks of stone. All were being careful, but one of them was working with an intensity and at a pace far beyond his colleagues. Each craftsman was asked in turn what he was doing. Each replied that he was working on the stone to make it into a building block. Finally, the craftsman who was working with some passion was asked what he was doing. He replied, "I'm helping to build a cathedral."

> It could, of course, been a mosque or a synagogue, or any building of artistic or spiritual worth. The point is that the enthusiastic craftsman had meaning in his work over and above the activities and processes involved in his day-to-day work. Leadership is about providing this extra dimension, so giving meaning to everyday tasks.

The second essence of leadership is that great leaders make their followers into leaders. They become the servants of their followers, and in so doing turn them into heroes and heroines. The Difference Deliverers are led by the Difference Drivers to act with more courage than they could possibly have imagined they possessed. The Polish shipyard workers following Lech Walesa, and the Indian followers of Mahatma Gandhi, showed huge courage, under severe provocation. This was courage they could not have found on their own, without the inspiration of leaders who made them feel both valued and powerful.

Although some cultures are still rooted in the management rather than the leadership paradigm, the trends towards increased democracy and increased affluence are both likely to lead to a decline in the rigidity and power of management hierarchies. Authority based on position or title will become less important as people are increasingly independent and want to think for themselves more. Leadership is thus a skill we will all need in more abundance as the century progresses.

> Leadership is a huge subject—too big to more than touch on here—but its essentials are based on serving, and adding value to other human beings. Creating a vision is really the ability to imagine a better tomorrow and give people hope—and the tools to achieve it. And leaders, if they are wise, will look to the needs of their followers first, rather than their own.

Indeed, making a difference and leadership are in many ways identical skills. Focusing on how you can help people, rather than what you can get out of them, is a basic requirement for the success of both.

Building people, and finding the best in them, rather than the worst, are core strengths. Equally important is the insight that confrontation can be a loving act. When the going gets tough, and things need to be said—especially when ground rules are being disregarded or broken—confronting those taking liberties can be the difference between long-term success or failure.

LEADERSHIP ADDS VALUE TO GLOBALIZATION

Globalization is an area where many people want to make a difference. Leadership—the ability to add value to people, either individually or in communities of interest—will play a crucial role in whether globalization can be made more of a creative force than it sometimes appears today.

Leaving aside the arguments as to whether the long-term benefits of increasing global wealth outweigh the disadvantages of some unprincipled exploitation of workers in the less developed world in the shorter term, there are two major fundamental changes to the status quo that good leadership—by both multinationals and individuals—is capable of delivering.

The first comes from the apparent improvement in the behavior of multinationals that source products in less developed countries, in which standards of employee conditions are different from those in the West. This improvement in behavior comes from several causes. One is the public outcry at such malpractices by consumers, and the public pillorying of leaders both in the media, and at annual results conferences.

This has made many of them sit up and take notice. While they had been content to follow their competitors and turn a blind eye to things that happened in far-off lands—because that was the status quo (everybody did it so it was all right)—now they realized that they were accountable, and their reputation was on the line.

In addition to the consumer demands about employment conditions for developing world workers, a significant movement has built up calling multinationals to account for what are seen as their unfair trading practices. Under severe global competitive pressures, companies have put what is seen as unfair pressure on suppliers—manufacturers, farmers, and so on—in order to hold down prices for the consumers in the countries they sell in.

Fair trade organizations have grown up, with the goal of making a difference to the status quo by giving suppliers—especially farmers—a better deal. Consumers in developed countries are responding positively, buying the fair trade products, putting more pressure on the multinationals—and in particular their leaders—to rethink their supply chain strategies.

Chief executives in the developed world have also come under further pressures from rapidly developing codes of corporate governance, which demand greater transparency and accountability. Both shareholders and consumers want to know what is going on within companies. When damaging information comes to light about the behavior of a company, especially a multinational, the Internet disseminates the information globally, at the speed of light.

The other major development in recent years as a demand on businesses to behave more responsibly is, of course, the environment. Taking resources, building and operating factories, and disposing of waste products with no thought for their environmental impact is no longer acceptable. There are now plenty of people and organizations that are prepared to blow the whistle if they discover it is going on.

For many of the chief executives these pressures are extremely unwelcome. They are unwelcome for a very simple reason. Global competition means that in most product areas, there is price deflation. Prices are going down, not up. This means that companies producing food products, electrical products, cars, clothing, and so on are getting lower revenues each year for the products they sell.

This challenge is compounded by the fact that the pressures for better behavior in the supply chain—not exploiting developing world suppliers, or using suppliers who do not care what conditions their workers operate in, disposing of their waste responsibility, as well as paying their own employees more each year as the competition for the best staff intensifies—all add to costs. So prices are going down, and marketing and distribution costs are going up—both with a relentless intensity.

Not only are margins and profitability being squeezed by costs going up, and the prices companies can charge going down, shareholders too want higher returns each year. For the most part, the shareholders are not the popular misconception of fat, greedy capitalists. The majority of shares are held by financial institutions like insurance companies and pension funds. As dependency ratios in developed countries deteriorate—too few young people supporting too many old people—and occupational pension schemes become unaffordable and are terminated, the private pension schemes are the chief source of pension provision for a growing percentage of the population.

As a significant percentage of the funds of pension providers is invested in stocks and shares, the performance of those stocks and shares is extremely important. The collapse in stock market prices after the dot.com boom decimated the pension schemes of many people retiring at that time, or soon after. So shareholder pressure for higher returns from large companies in the world's stock markets is not greed feeding on greed, but need feeding on need.

Chief executives of companies of all sizes thus have significant and real pressures on them from all angles. In terms of environmental responsibility, fair trade, and ethical sourcing policies, many react by getting better at improving their presentation of the facts, and making cosmetic improvements wherever they are necessary. They pay convenient lip service to the demands for them to demonstrate more honorable behavior as global citizens.

The good news however, is that a small but increasing number are beginning to see the situation as an opportunity for them to make a personal difference. I personally know several who fall into this category. They do this for two reasons. One is that they, as individuals, believe in better corporate citizenship, and see it as a chance to add, rather than take, value. They understand as individuals that the planet's resources are at risk, and the need to behave sustainably is urgent and important. In addition, they too have families, with children agitating for improvements in corporate behavior, and often find their own offspring a tougher audience than even the environmental activists.

The second reason is that they can see the way the wind is blowing. As individuals move up Maslow's hierarchy of needs through increased affluence, they are more aware of the issues we are discussing. They are also becoming more demanding and assertive—they want to improve things, to make a difference. As a result, people—what they think, and how they feel about your company—are becoming more and more important to businesses and organizations of all kinds.

It is rapidly becoming apparent in business that people are the key to the future. This importance comes in two dimensions. First, people make up the consumers, employees, suppliers, and shareholders of a company, and therefore have its success or failure in its hands.

Employees care as much as consumers about the behavior of the organization they work for.

They want to work for organizations that behave well, and produce ethical and sustainable products and services. Increasingly the best people—particularly the young—will only work for companies who behave well, and have leadership that is visionary, and genuinely committed to improving the world as well as making profits. They leave companies where this is not the case, and go to competitors who walk the walk, rather than talking the talk. Why would they want to create value, and make a difference in their private lives, and not want to carry it over into their work lives?

Second, there has been a significant shift in the major levers of wealth creation. In the nineteenth and twentieth centuries wealth creation was mainly predicated on the access to both raw materials and capital. Capital, in particular, was crucial to be able to build and fund steel mills, factories, stock, and so on—all the things required to build business empires.

In the twenty-first century manufactured things are less important. In most developed societies services now make up about 80 percent of gross domestic product—far outweighing the importance of manufacturing or agriculture. This is less so, of course, in developing countries, as much of the manufacturing activity has been shifted to them. But in developing countries too, services are becoming more important, as services like IT, call centers, and so on are outsourced to them.

The point is that services are coming more and more to dominate economies, and services, by and large, are not large devourers of capital. Microsoft, one of the largest companies in the world, was set up on a capital base of less than $50,000. And it only went public on the stock exchange to make its founders rich, rather than—as would historically have been the case—to generate capital to fund expansion.

What services need is not capital, but good people. They are only as good as their employees. Full-service airlines need planes to fly, but the planes, more or less, are all the same. It is the care and commitment of the staff—the so-called customer experience—that differentiates one airline from another.

Even more important is attracting, and keeping, good people with good ideas. It is good ideas that make the difference. Companies stay ahead by innovating—creating new value for their customers.

New ideas create wealth. The wheels on the suitcase meant that many people went out and bought a new suitcase, increasing the volume within the market hugely. The invention of products like the Sony Walkman, or the Apple iPod developed new markets, by creating significant new value for customers. Information technology consultants, fitness trainers in gyms, practitioners in many branches of alternative medicine, are services that add significant value, but didn't exist 10 or 20 years ago. A need was identified, the new value was created (usually requiring very little capital), and a whole new service sector was created.

So chief executives with vision and insight understand how profoundly important people are to their continued success. Not just in their roles as consumers, suppliers, and shareholders, but now, as employees, providing a source both of future wealth creation and of great service to build that wealth.

Committed, enthusiastic staff, who identify with the purpose of the company (how the chief executive articulates the meaning of what the company does) will create a whole lot more value for customers than unmotivated staff who are waiting to clock off, so they can go home, and make a difference in their private lives.

IDEAS ENABLE INDIVIDUALS TO CREATE HUGE VALUE AND MAKE BIG DIFFERENCES

Human talent may have taken over from capital as the chief lever of creating of economic value, but it still needs leadership by the human beings involved to make great ideas happen. The good news is that it opens way for value creation and leadership at far more levels, and to far greater effect.

The absence of the need to raise capital to start a company or organization releases all sorts of energies. All you need to start with is an idea—and if it's a non-profit organization, some like-minded people—and you're off. You then need persistence (courage) to blast through all the setbacks and wrong turnings that are part of building any enterprise. Finally, you need leadership skills (which include courage) to make sure others can understand the excitement of your vision, and the relevance of the value you intend to create, so they can be part of making it happen.

One outstanding example of this process is the Grameen bank. The story of the bank is a tale of someone who decided he had an urgent need to create value for those around him, became a Difference Driver, recruited Difference Deliverers, and changed the world for the poor in Bangladesh.

In 1974, Muhammad Yunus had returned to his native Chittagong in Bangladesh after a Fulbright scholarship in the United States, where he had gained a PhD in economics at Vanderbilt University, Nashville, Tennessee. He had been appointed head of the economics department at Chittagong University. There was a famine on at the time, and whenever he walked outside of the campus he saw skeletal people, waiting for death. The jarring dissonance between their poverty, and the theories of conventional economics he was teaching, deeply unsettled him.

Why, he asked himself, was conventional economics so powerless in the face of such deprivation? He got talking to an old woman who was selling bamboo stools, and finally asked her how much profit she was making on each stool. It turned out she was making the equivalent of 2 US cents, after paying 20 cents for the bamboo, and paying a money lender at a rate sometimes as high as 10 percent per *week*. In reality she was a bonded slave to the moneylender, with no chance of breaking out of the circle of slave labor and debt.

Yunus determined to do something—anything—to save at least one human life by coming up with some sort of solution that could break the vicious circle. He sent one of his students to the village the woman came from to find out how many others there were like her, and how much their total debt to the moneylenders was. The student reported back that 42 people were in debt and the sum of all the loans they owed totaled $27. Yunus felt ashamed to be part of a society and an economic system that could not provide $27 for 42 hard working and skilled people.

He took the money from his pocket, gave it to the student, and told him to give it to those needing it, making sure that they understood it was a loan, and should be paid back when they could afford it.

The villagers were enraptured, which set Yunus thinking. This seed corn money could not only help them survive, it could also fan the spark of personal initiative and enterprise that could pull them out of poverty. Could he therefore persuade a conventional bank to lend to these people? He tried the local branch of the bank on the university campus, where he was met with derision—he must know that these villagers were untrustworthy, and besides, they had no collateral.

Then began the familiar story of the hard work really starting, as he attempted to turn the idea into a workable reality. It needed character and courage in abundance, as Yunus took the idea to other banks, to senior people in them, and eventually only succeeded because he personally guaranteed the loans. He was continually told that the borrowers would not repay them. They did. Despite all the advice to the contrary, he carried on giving out his "micro loans," personally guaranteeing them to the bank.

Finally, fed up with all the hassle, he hit on the idea of his own bank. The government was resistant, but after two years of negotiation, in 1983, the Grameen Bank (literally village bank) was formed. Since 1983 it has now cumulatively loaned almost **$5 billion**. It now has well over 1500 branches, which service over 53,000 villages in Bangladesh, as well as supporting banks in 58 other countries, including the United States, Canada, France, and the Netherlands.

The whole enterprise is impressive in all respects, but two figures perhaps stand out from all the rest. The first is that **94 percent of the loans are to women**. The second is that over **98 percent of the loans are repaid**, a figure much higher than conventional banks.

Yunus didn't stop there. He has since moved on from micro loans to other areas. These include what is termed a "struggling member program." Struggling member is a more positive name for beggar. Struggling members' loans are already enabling many borrowers to raise themselves out of begging for a living.

Another imaginative and empowering innovation is the phone lady program. Yunus understands how telephony can supercharge economic development. Individuals buy mobile phones with a loan from the bank, and calls are subsidized. The purchasers, many of whom are "struggling members," then sell on the calls for a slightly higher price. Already 68,000 villages now have a phone they can use, and the plan is eventually to distribute 100 million mobile phones into rural areas.

The Grameen Bank already accounts for over 1 percent of the gross domestic product of Bangladesh. It has empowered countless underprivileged and vulnerable people, and taken them out of poverty. In the words of the World Bank, "It has allowed millions of individuals to work their way out of poverty with dignity."

All this from one man, without significant capital, but a great idea, determined to create value for others, and make a difference.

7

Where we meet Lee and Helen, who are searching for their purpose

One of the significant insights that emerge from Muhammad Yunus's heroic achievements in creating and developing the Grameen Bank and its offshoots is that he did not start out with a vision.

If you had asked him what his purpose was back in 1974, when he returned to Chittagong University, he would have probably said, "To be a good teacher." He had no vision—he was an economist, after all. It was conscience that provided him with his purpose. His compassion for those suffering and starving around him—even though he was relatively isolated from it within the university campus—was what motivated him to undertake his uplifting and empowering work amongst the poor of Bangladesh. His conscience forced him to respond to the challenge of Edmund Burke's statement at the opening of the book:

> All that is necessary for the triumph of evil is for good men to do nothing.

This does not, however, let us off the hook in attempting to define our purpose, and map our values. It may be that the future-defining event or situation like the one that occurred to Yunus does not happen to us. So it's back to Schwarz's *The Magic of Thinking Big*: if the spirit doesn't move you, sit down and move your spirit.

In order to help you move your spirit, and to reprise some of the earlier concepts before moving on to the specifics of the Make a Difference Mindset, I'm going to take the example of two fictional characters. These characters—Lee and Helen— will go through the exercises to discover their purpose, and map their values, and will then go on to find ways of fulfilling that purpose and making a difference.

The reason I do this, in a sense, is to walk the talk. I find books that provide theories without practical examples very frustrating. As the Make a Difference Mindset is a new theory, as it were (so there are no case histories), providing fictional examples of it in action may go some way to dramatizing what it is about, and even, to a small degree, confirming its effectiveness.

So a short bit of background on our intrepid difference makers. Lee is in his late 30s, and in terms of ability is a high-flyer, but is not flying as high as he should be. He wears a light two-piece khaki suit, thin-wired spectacles, has gelled hair, and looks a smart operator.

He *is* a smart operator, but is frustrated his abilities are not recognized more by the corporation he works for, which is a large mobile phone company. In fact, Lee is talented, but more than that, he has genuine insight into how companies work, and how to make them work better. His strategic grasp of markets and cultures is remarkable in one not in senior management.

He is better than many of the high-flyers that work for him, or whom he works for. He has a keen desire to prove himself. He is very clear that at this stage in his life, his chosen domain for making a difference is in his job. He wants to show his fellow workers, his bosses—and his family, to which he is deeply attached—that he is effective and successful.

So he wants to make a difference at work by creating new value for the corporation that will be recognized and rewarded. He feels time is dribbling away, and that if he doesn't produce something which will make a difference and be recognized soon, more and more of his younger colleagues will be passing him on their way to the top of the company. He is inhibited from being more successful by office politics. He refuses to join in the machinations, and feels out of tune with the recently appointed chief executive (CEO), who seems not to buy into the founding ideals of the company.

Another of Lee's challenges is that he has to find more time for his family in his busy day than most of his colleagues do. Many of them aren't married yet; so don't have the responsibilities that Lee does. He quite often leaves on time (unlike many of his colleagues), but takes work home, so he can keep up with the requirements of his job. He finds this makes him very tired, and by the weekend he has to draw on all his reserves of energy to be bouncy and interactive with his young children. Despite his time pressures, he still finds time once a month to do voluntary work for a large charity.

In deciding to give the Make a Difference Mindset a go, he is at first resistant to the crucial first stage of defining his purpose. He feels he knows his purpose—to be successful and earn lots of money, so he can give his family financial security. On reflection he realizes that to make a discernible difference he is going to need to find either more than 24 hours in the day, or some new energy from somewhere. Understanding his purpose may be a source of this energy, so he goes ahead and does the exercise.

Before we look at Lee's efforts to define his purpose, let's meet Helen. Helen is in her late 20s, highly paid, and living a very successful lifestyle. She is medium height, dark haired, and attractive, particularly when she smiles (which is not as often as it should be). Underneath her success, she is feeling not just the internal clock ticking away, but also a sense of "is this all there is?" She is a corporate lawyer. While she finds the work intellectually stimulating, and the adrenaline buzz of the big deals she works on exciting, she has a sense that she is not engaging in her work emotionally, and it's beginning to feel a bit sterile.

She has a difficult relationship with her parents. When they were divorced six or seven years ago, she felt hurt and abandoned. She has never outgrown the feeling of resentment towards their new partners, and towards her new siblings. She feels guilty at herself for this, but the pressures of her job—sometimes working through the night to complete deals—mean she has little time for bridge building.

LEE AND HELEN: FINDING THE DEFINING THREAD

Lee began to reflect on his purpose, taking some time to answer the two questions, "What do I really like to do?" and "What areas of my life do I get most satisfaction from?"

He was surprised to find both questions difficult. He had no major passions in his life. He had been a good badminton player, and had loved the game, but has not been able to keep it up, through pressures of work and family. He had loved going

to the theatre and the cinema, but again these had wilted somewhat for the same reason. He loved his family, and enjoyed
being with them, but by Monday morning was quite relieved to
get back to the mental stimulus of his work. He was very keen
to see his children fulfill their potential, but he saw this as a
team effort between himself, his wife, his wider family, and the
children's teachers.

As he jotted down the wisps of feelings that came to him as
he pondered over purpose in the days that followed, one or two
threads began to emerge. He felt good that he worked for a
mobile phone operator, because mobile phones enhance life.
They enable human beings to communicate more effectively
with each other, in both their working and social lives. He
hadn't thought about it before in these terms, but he felt that
his work had more of a worthwhile purpose as a result of this
insight.

He also began to feel frustrated on two fronts following this
new perception. The first was that he felt that the company he
worked for did not understand the bigger picture of what it was
doing. He thought that this was possibly the result of several
changes of ownership, which had left both the management
and employees without any long-term sense of either stability
or direction. This had been compounded by the arrival of the
new CEO, who was out of sympathy with the history of the
company. The second was a direct result of this. There was
widespread cynicism within the company about the changes,
and a distrust of management that made his day-to-day work
even more challenging than it already was.

He wasn't sure what all this meant as to his purpose, but he
felt, nonetheless, that he was making some progress. He therefore decided to move on to the next stage. He photocopied the
list of values from the Values Map, and started to examine it.

Looking down the list of values he found it easy to select his
top 10, which, in alphabetical order (i.e. not in any order of
priority) were:

Enthusiasm—he was an enthusiast, and valued the quality in
others.

Family—the lynchpin to everything he did.

Friends—very important, he just wished he could see them more often.

Work/life balance—something he fought to maintain, despite the pressures.

Honesty—even under pressure, he couldn't lie, and hated others lying.

Meaning—he had a growing sense of spirituality, and was searching for it.

Openness—he was very open, and was uncomfortable when others weren't.

Pride—in the positive sense of being proud of his family and his company.

Reward—he was keen on reward, for both family security and recognition.

Status—honesty as one of his values meant he had to admit to this.

He wasn't totally happy circling status, but he felt he had to recognize his feeling of under-achievement. He wanted his colleagues and his friends to know that he was a high-flyer, even if his career to date didn't seem to confirm this.

Reflecting further, he felt one key area of his values was missing. He searched around for something in the list that included it, but couldn't find anything. He therefore added an eleventh value—sharing information/knowledge. He was passionate about telling people what was going on—in making them feeling involved in whatever it was he was doing at work, or with his family and friends. He resented his bosses holding out on him, and only discovering later information that might have enabled him to do a better job, or not make an avoidable mistake.

He knew the word communications was a more conventional and concise definition of sharing information/knowledge, but he felt it was an overused word, and, as a result, did not have the clarity he needed to define the value.

His next step was to rank his values in terms of importance for him. This took some time, and he changed the ranking several times. Even when he had finished, he wasn't totally satisfied that he had the order right. He left it a day or so, and when he came back to it, he changed it again. Finally (or not finally, he suspected) the order of priority came out as follows:

1. Family
2. Honesty
3. Openness
4. Reward
5. Sharing information/knowledge
6. Enthusiasm
7. Pride
8. Meaning
9. Work/life balance
10. Friends
11. Status

As he proceeded to draw up his Values Map—his engineer's training made it both colorful and beautifully symmetrical— he discovered a further prioritization going on, almost subconsciously. The map was the shape of an elegant, elongated triangle—an extended arrowhead—with a small tail at the bottom.

Family was at the apex of the arrow's head. As the triangle widened slightly, honesty and openness were side by side. Next level down came reward, sharing information/ knowledge, and enthusiasm, and the widest part of the giant arrowhead was made up of pride, meaning, work/life balance, and friends. Status formed the small tail at the bottom.

Looking at his artistic masterpiece, he saw that it was the top six that really excited him—in the priority that his map had put on them. Family was out in front. Honesty and openness were close behind, and reward, sharing information/knowledge, and enthusiasm were a step behind them. Each of them struck a chord within him, so that when he thought of any of them being threatened or compromised, he could feel anger beginning to rise within him. He hadn't realized it consciously, but these were all things he was passionate about.

He found this very helpful, and he was delighted to have located magnetic north, but it still didn't give him true north, his purpose. He therefore moved on to the next stage, which is writing the three obituaries.

Lee sat down to write, and at first found it very difficult. His mind went blank, and he could think of nothing to put in the obituaries. Eventually, as he began to write, he picked up speed, and ideas came out, seemingly from nowhere, some of which took him by surprise.

Obituary supposedly written by his eldest child aged 9

My Dad was a kind man. He sometimes lost his temper, but it didn't last long, and he always said he was sorry. I felt it wasn't always me he was angry at, but I wasn't sure.

He often seemed tired, but he nearly always managed to see us once a day, either when we got up, or before we went to bed. He was always around at weekends, and didn't go off playing golf like a lot of his friends did. They would phone him up to ask him to play, but he always said no—he had some important things to sort out. And he winked at us as he said it.

He liked reading us books, and explaining how things worked. He seemed to know about things, and didn't get impatient when we didn't understand them first time. He used to get very excited explaining things. Sometimes we'd ask him questions, just to see him get excited, so we could get excited too.

Dad was a champion badminton player when he was young, but he didn't keep it up. He taught us the game, and we loved playing it with him. He was still fit for a man as old as 38.

What I'll most miss about Dad is his laugh. It didn't happen very often, and it wasn't very loud, but when it did happen, it took everyone along with it. We children would laugh and laugh too, even when we didn't know what we were laughing about, which was most of the time.

Lee was beginning to get emotional writing his imaginary obituary from his child, so he changed tack, and moved on the next one, from, in his case, his wife.

Obituary supposedly written by his wife

When we met, Lee was full of hope, and full of fun. He retained these qualities throughout his life, despite his work situation making it increasingly difficult to keep them up.

He has been a wonderful husband and father. He was a great explainer of things to the children. We all remember his explaining the internal combustion engine to us. He had us all shouting "Yes" for the accelerator being pushed down. We then all clapped our hands to describe the spark from the spark plug exploding. He then had us pumping our arms and legs to simulate the pistons starting to rotate the crankshaft. Finally, we had to go round the room, clapping, pumping, shouting, running faster and faster, till we all collapsed in a heap, laughing till we cried.

He worked very hard, and put a lot of his heart, as well as his brain, into the business. I know he must have been very tired at times, but seldom showed it. He didn't talk much about it, but I had the feeling that he wasn't appreciated as he should have been by the organization he worked for. All wives feel that, I'm sure, but in Lee's case, I think it was true.

He was a kind and generous man. He was patient and caring with my father, who developed early onset Parkinson's disease, and helped my mother and my sisters cope for a long time with a very difficult situation. He had a very strong sense of family, and was there for people.

Lee was a good man. We will miss him.

He moved on to the third, and last obituary.

Obituary supposedly written by P, Lee's friend and colleague at work

Lee was an enthusiast, and good with young staff. He encouraged them, and made sure they had a vision of the company as it was when it was pioneering the thinking, as well as the technology, in the industry.

He was generally popular at work, and even the mockers couldn't diminish his enthusiasm. He had a good understanding of the company, and its potential in the market it operates in, and had a broader perspective than most of his contemporaries. His contribution to the success of the business was significant. He made things happen, which is a rare attribute at any level of business.

Unfortunately, changes of ownership meant that his contribution wasn't universally recognized. The CEO, in particular, felt that Lee was trying to put the clock back, not forward. He tended to see Lee as someone standing in his way, rather than helping him build the business.

Lee was particularly strong at innovation, not only finding ideas for new products or services but discovering new ways of doing things. Unusually for an engineer, he was very good with people, and was at his best resolving conflicts and building teams.

He enjoyed tilting at windmills, trying to change the culture, and by many of us he was admired all the more for that. For other members of management, he seemed to be digging a deeper and deeper hole for himself. Sadly he now lies in that hole.

Lee permitted himself this rather sick joke, because he felt a sudden sense of release. He was at last getting some real insight into his situation, and his frustrations. Writing them down had brought his generalized dissatisfactions into sharp focus. He could now see more clearly what the issues were.

What he had thought was lack of recognition, lack of status, was actually a sense of fear by most of the management that his nostalgia for the company's past, coupled with his active promoting of the previous leadership's values of openness and a vision of the company's role in society, were encouraging confusion amongst the staff as to what the company now stood for (which essentially was a strong bottom line).

He had thought he was viewed as a builder, a company enthusiast. But he was probably viewed as someone who was subversive: someone potentially dangerous, and to be watched. The colleague, P, from whose point of view the obituary was written, was a very senior manager, in charge of operations for the whole region. Coming to think of it, because P shared many of Lee's views and values—the reason they got on so well—he too was probably under threat.

P was very good at his job, but no one was safe. Lee remembered a recent conversation with P when he had put his arm round Lee's shoulder and said, with a twinkle in his eye, "We're an endangered species, Lee, but we can't give up the good fight!" Lee, being an enthusiast, had paid more heed to the second part of the sentence, but he now saw that the first part probably carried equal weight in P's mind.

Over the next few days and weeks Lee thought more and more about exactly what the "good fight" was, because he realized this was what he was passionate about, and this could become his purpose.

Lee's letter

The letter, you may recall, is written to a young friend who is on the same wavelength as you, with similar values, and it describes your achievements and life lessons—from the perspective of you as a 75-year-old.

Dear C (his 19 year old nephew, with whom he had a very good relationship),

Thanks for your letter. Glad to hear things are going well. I'm writing to you, almost from beyond the grave, as 75 seems an enormous age to reach.

I am delighted and flattered that you have asked for my advice. As I reflect on my life, which has turned out to be successful—and certainly fulfilling—I can see that certain lessons stand out. The most important is to find the core you— what you stand for—and then be true to it. Integrity is another word for it. If you retain your integrity, you can face all manner of challenges. If you compromise it, you will be quickly over-whelmed by events, because you won't know who you are or what you're about.

I had one major event in my life that confirmed my complete belief in this. It was when I was trying to improve the culture of the company I was working for—it had become very cynical—and I had a confrontation with the top management over the issue. It could have gone either way, but fortunately they backed me, and gave me the tools to do something about it. Had I crumpled under the pressure to compromise my beliefs, my life would have been very different, and I suspect the company would have turned out very differently.

After the decision to back me, we made a few mistakes, and it took time, but eventually we turned the culture round—and a better financial bottom line resulted in subsequent years. I took the lessons I learned and applied them in other organizations, fortunately with considerable success. This is the second piece of advice. Contrary to popular belief, most people working for organizations of all sorts want to work hard, bring more of their talents and enthusiasm to work, and find some meaning in it. If you can find a way to help this happen, it's a win/win all round. Customers, employees—the stakeholders—get a higher return both in value and satisfaction.

The next important message from your old uncle is to be enthusiastic, no matter what. Without being immodest, I believe one of my strongest talents (and I've had to work very hard at it sometimes) is my enthusiasm. I love what I do, and that infects those around me. People know I'm excited by what I'm doing and they get excited too.

So hang on to that wonderful enthusiasm of yours. You'll find as life begins to bite—job, family, responsibilities, and so on—there are times when you won't feel so enthusiastic. There will be people and situations aplenty that will seem set to hoover up your excitement with life, and suck the positive mood out of you. Resist. Don't, as they say, let the bastards get you down.

Not only will they try to obliterate your enthusiasm, they will try to poison any positive initiative you try to take. Again, resist. Life's poisoners rejoice in their ability to blacken everyone and everything around them with their own life-denying attitudes. Carry on regardless. Your positive values are life-enhancing—theirs are toxic.

My work over the past 40 years has been involved in creating positive, life-enhancing cultures, so I know what I am talking about. If care isn't taken to avoid it, toxic cultures can grow up in any organization—nowhere is safe. They can even occur in charities. I've seen charities where the people working there are well intentioned, but sometimes new, dynamic managers come in to take the charity on to the next level of size and significance, and the old guard resist coming on board to the new vision.

They are determined to defend the old ways of doing things against any new enthusiast who comes in and tries to change things. Because profit is not a consideration, this sort of internal paralysis can take a very long time to show up, as no one is seen to be responsible for efficiency and effectiveness.

This is why I now work free for several charities. On the face of it, they call me in to assist in fundraising efforts, but my work lies in advising them on how to make their cultures more open, and dynamic.

My last piece of advice to you is to get on the front foot, and lead the charge for your style of openness and your values. Become a leader, and inspire people with your enthusiasm. People will follow you because you know what you're about, and you'll give them hope.

Have a great life,
Uncle Lee

Lee sat and looked at the letter. He was slightly out of breath. He had started slowly, but once going, it had started to flow, and he was amazed at how quickly it all came out. He still wasn't sure what it all meant for his purpose, but he felt a lot of useful stuff that would help him find it was coming out.

He was getting excited—he felt he was close to something that could be very useful in helping him find the course he should take.

HELEN SEARCHES FOR PURPOSE

When Helen eventually got home from work it was after 10 o'clock. She was profoundly tired (she had worked through the previous night) but knew she wouldn't be able to sleep until the adrenaline rushing around in her veins had subsided a bit. She showered, felt joy at having clean hair for the first time in what seemed like a week, but was probably only two or three days. She made herself a snack in the kitchen of her flat. All the fresh vegetables, fruits, and salads had withered in their containers, as she had not had time to shop for days.

Although she had one or two details to clear up in the morning, the deal was done. She felt relief, but little sense of satisfaction or achievement. So another large deal had been tied up. Having met both the parties involved several times, she had a feeling the logic of the deal was money driven, not market driven. The customers wouldn't benefit, and certainly the employees would be significant losers. The shareholders might or might not benefit—mergers often didn't add much value. The certain winners were the financial and legal advisors—of which she was one—and some of the management, who had incentive schemes and contracts, which meant they won either way.

As she picked at her food, she found herself feeling empty. Not only empty, but lonely, too. Her job prevented her from keeping up with her family on a regular basis, so a call from her at this hour would be seen as a pretty heavy call for help.

She couldn't go on like this. The money and the challenge of her job were fine, but there was very little else. The social usefulness of what she was doing she felt was pretty marginal. She didn't really like most of her clients, and while some of her colleagues were fine, she spent too much time with them working to want to spend more time socializing with them.

Helen had always had a strong social conscience, but had suppressed it when choosing a career. Since her parents' divorce she had been determinedly independent. She had no intention of asking either of them for financial support, so she had chosen a career that ensured a high income, and the possibility in the longer term of financial independence. She was still far short of financial independence, but was certainly comfortably off for someone her age. She had no thoughts of marriage, although she didn't rule it out, and had not had a boyfriend of any longevity since leaving university.

She knew she was at a turning point, but had no idea where to turn. The one thing she did know was that this would mean changing her job. She had had these thoughts before, and had done nothing about it. This time it would be different. Ruefully she remembered she had said that to herself before too.

She thought about what she might do. The thought of making a more positive contribution to society—making a difference—appealed to her. At this stage she had no idea what domains of her life might be affected. She was clear that she had to change her job, but as to whether this meant having a job that enabled her to do something worthwhile in her spare time, or having a job that was intrinsically worthwhile, she had no views on.

So she began at the beginning. She set out, there and then, to start the work of defining her purpose. She addressed the questions, "What do I really like to do?" and "What areas of my life do I get most satisfaction from?" She wrote out both questions on a piece of paper, and stared at them.

As she stared at the sheet, she began to feel a rising sense of alarm close to panic. The answer to the second question was: "There are no areas of my life I get satisfaction from." Everything that gave her joy had dried up. Turning from such distressing thoughts, she decided to find the answer to the first question, which seemed possibly more fruitful.

What she really would like to do at the moment was to grab a couple of days at a health spa to get some physical regeneration, tranquility, and pampering. She realized for her, at this stage of her life, this was hedonism rooted in escapism. It had been well earned, but was an antidote to her toxic lifestyle, rather than a reward for the efforts of a busy and fulfilling life. She vowed that next time she went to a health farm or spa, it would be as a reward, not an escape.

As a child, and at university she had been involved in both golf and tennis, and had represented her university at the latter.

She hardly played either now. She still went to the gym when she could, but this was defensive, avoiding health breakdown, rather than building a healthy and radiant body. She had enjoyed reading, but again, nowadays hardly picked up a novel, and seldom read the newspapers beyond the legal and business pages.

One previous passion that had almost entirely shriveled for her was politics. She had been—unusually for a lawyer—very left-wing at university. Her interest in politics had been aroused in a gap year between school and her degree studies. She had worked in an orphanage in a country burdened by debt taken out by previous profligate and corrupt rulers, who had since been deposed. She had found working with the children very rewarding, and had returned with a mission to work towards reducing poverty and suffering around the world.

Sadly, towards the end of her second year of studying law, and enjoying the cut and thrust of student politics, her parents had dropped their bombshell. After 30 years of marriage, they were divorcing. They had waited for her to establish herself at university, and complete her second year exams, and then told her. They thought the timing would be good for her. In fact it was terrible.

Ruining the after-exam celebrations was a minor concern against the hurt of the event, and the knowledge she had no true home to go to in the holidays. The house she had lived in all her life was already on the market. Fresh starts, with, she thought they intimated, fresh partners, were being made by both her mother and her father. Plenty of her friends had divorced parents, but it seemed worse for her, as she only had one sister—who was married with a young family—to share the pain with.

Her final year at university had been more concerned with solving her own, rather than the world's problems. She moved on to law school to finish her legal qualifications, and the pressure of study had meant little or no time for political engagement.

So reflecting on "what do I really like to do?" she wrote **"help young people,"** and then **"fight for the downtrodden."**

Seeing these words on the paper, it was as if a small light had been turned on in her head. She felt she had made some progress.

Tiredness now began to overwhelm her. She decided to leave the next step till the following night, and went to bed elated, with more hope than she had had for a very long time.

The following evening she moved on to the Values Map. She looked at the list for a long time, then circled the following 10 values (in alphabetical, non-hierarchical order):

Community service—important to her, though it had lapsed since leaving university.

Friends—again important, though under-serviced.

Humor/fun—again, she wanted to rediscover her high-spirited, amusing self.

Kindness—nothing upset her more than seeing people behave unkindly.

Independence—a value almost forced upon her, but one now highly treasured.

Integrity—a value she refused to compromise despite some clients wanting to take short cuts to get deals done.

Meaning—something she now realized she was searching for very seriously.

Perseverance—a value she believed in, and delivered on.

Physical exercise—she had let it slip a bit, but she still believed in the principle of a healthy mind in a healthy body.

Social responsibility—though stunted, it was still an important value for her.

Helen had passionately wanted to add family to her list of values, but she felt that this was a gut value she wanted to redevelop, rather than one she currently held.

She realized that one or two of her other values—like humor/fun, and community service—weren't too current either, but she knew these were values that she had not only held all her life, but could resuscitate relatively quickly. She knew she would have to address family, but that it would take time.

What struck her most about her list of values was how she was under-performing on so many in her current situation. Seeing this cemented her resolve to change the situation. Without the list, she might well have woken up the following morning, dismissed her current mood as the result of tiredness and stress, and continued on as before. Seeing how half her values—and her personality—had been shriveled by her job confirmed her resolve to change things.

So Helen progressed to the next step of ranking her 10 selected values in terms of importance. She thought this would take no time at all, but she had to think long and hard over the position of one or two of them. Here's the ranked list:

1. Meaning
2. Integrity
3. Friends
4. Kindness
5. Community service
6. Humor/fun
7. Physical exercise
8. Social Responsibility
9. Independence
10. Perseverance

She was surprised that independence and perseverance came out so low, but then realized these were things that had been important because of the events in her life—and she had become strong in—but that they would possibly be less central to her from now on.

When she moved on to do her very colorful Values Map (she made it look like a rocket with speed lines coming off the sides) she put meaning at the apex of the arrow (or in her case, the rocket's tip), with integrity, friends, and kindness just below, forming the rest of the arrowhead (or lead portion of the rocket). She put family in brackets, just underneath these four leading values. She reflected that when she came to do her Values Map again in a few months time, she hoped family would be there with its brackets removed.

She had already learned that her values and life needed reshaping. Magnetic north, let alone true north, was a long way from where she was at the moment. Having meaning as a top value was really a cry for help to herself to bring some back into her existence.

She made herself a light supper with the fresh food she had purchased at the shop on the way home, and then moved on to start the three obituaries. She had already had a good session at the gym, and felt glowing with health and hope. She fixed herself a fruit drink (it was her first alcohol-free day in some weeks) and sat down to write.

Obituary supposedly written by M, her nephew, aged 18

Helen once heard me telling a friend she was cool. She tapped me on the shoulder, and said, "I'm not trying to be cool." That's the whole point. People who try to be cool never are, and Helen was cool because she could connect with us from when we were kids, and right through our young teenage years (when we thought we were super cool, but really didn't know what day of the week it was).

She was great to be with, and we looked forward to seeing her. She was amusing, and had a great knack of mimicking other people's voices. She used to wind me up by ringing me on my mobile and pretending to be me. I hope I don't really sound like that.

She helped me a lot during my exams. I get a bit worked up during exams—I hate them—but she could calm me down, and get me back to studying. She turned out to be right—I did do well in them.

I'll remember her most for making us laugh—especially in situations when we were trying to be serious. Recently, she seemed to have grown up a bit, and got a bit dull. Pity. Before that, although she was about 10 years older, she always seemed to be one of us kids.

She was a great aunt, and we'll miss her.

Having no husband or partner, Helen chose John, a friend from university, whom she saw whenever she could, as the second obituary writer.

Obituary supposedly written by John, a close friend

Helen was good at life—she had so much to give. She could make people of all ages feel good about themselves, but wasted her talents in an area of the law that seemed to value adversarial skills, rather than communication or caring skills. She had a strong talent to make people laugh.

At the end of the first year at university, I remember her being part of a very good cabaret evening in college. In one sketch she was playing the part of the then (male) prime minister, whose voice she managed to take off perfectly. The sketch was hilarious, and consisted of her explaining why she was introducing the new post of minister for harlots. The idea behind it was that prostitution was not only the oldest profession, but also the oldest service industry. As the country need service industries to replace our disappearing manufacturing industries, here was an opportunity for us to become world class. I don't remember many of the jokes, but I do recall that she finished the sketch with the line, "If, I may paraphrase our new minister's slogan, thank you for coming."

Above all, she was kind (again not something highly esteemed as a talent in corporate law). She was especially kind to me when I had an accident that meant I couldn't play football any more. She knew how much it meant to me, and dealt with it with sensitivity and humor. I wish I could have returned the favor when her parents divorced, but she resisted any support, from anywhere. She seemed determined to live with the pain, and even to nurture it.

She was kind, too, to other law students who struggled a bit to come to grips with the subject. She would patiently explain the principles involved—and give amusing examples of them in practice. Her impromptu lessons for desperate fellow law students helped many of them scrape through exams, which otherwise they might not have passed.

For her own legal career, the branch of the law she chose to pursue again seemed perverse. As young idealistic politicians we were fighting to bring about debt relief, and for some softening of the effects of globalization. In going into corporate law, where she was effectively helping multinationals gobble each other up more efficiently she seemed to be helping them to sharpen their claws, rather than file down their talons.

Her death is particularly untimely. She seemed at university, when I first met her to, be a flower that would blossom profusely, but since then she has seemed determined to stay as a bud and resist her flowering.

Helen sighed deeply, and moved on to her third, and last obituary.

Obituary supposedly written by K, a colleague at work

Helen was a good lawyer. She could have been a great lawyer, but not in the branch of law she chose. I don't know who advised her to be a corporate lawyer, but it wasn't very good advice.

She was technically very good, and she handled clients very well, but her heart didn't seem to be in it. She was close to being made a partner, but probably wouldn't have made it. Not through any lack of skill, but from a lack of deep-down commitment, which only tended to surface when a deal was finished, the client had gone, and we were all relaxing in a bar. She would drop her persona as a serious lawyer, and would make jokes that were very funny, but showed a deep lack of respect for the process we were all involved in.

She was very helpful to trainees and young lawyers, and indeed frequently provided social counseling for older lawyers, and I include myself in that number. She was non-judgmental, and very supportive. Which was somewhat surprising as, from what I have gleaned of her personal life, she had judged her parents fairly harshly.

Helen's greatest gift was her ability as a lawyer—and as a person—to understand where people were coming from, and to get quickly to the underlying individual concerns of the people she was dealing with. Often these concerns weren't the issues they were arguing about. She discerned, rightly, that what they were arguing about was a smokescreen for something else entirely. She had a knack of getting to the heart of the real objections, and resolving them. Once they were resolved, all the other objections melted away.

She was a great girl, and a good lawyer, and we'll miss her.

Before writing this, Helen had sometimes suspected that she would not be made a partner, but could now see that she almost certainly wouldn't, as a firm of that standing would have been very unlikely to take the risk. More fundamentally, it was now clear to her that she was a fish out of water, whereas just a few days ago she had been head down, working towards a partnership.

Helen's letter

The young person on the same wavelength as her to whom she chose to write was her 18-year-old goddaughter, to whom she was very close. Shuddering at the thought at how much she needed to accomplish by the time she was 75, she began to write.

She found the new perspective, given her by writing the letter from a point many years in the future, released several insights that she had previously suppressed.

My Darling Z,

Thanks for your letter, and I would be delighted to distil some of the insights I have gained over my now long life, if you think that would help you. There were times, particularly in my 20s, when I could have benefited from some advice myself, although, I have to confess, I was so screwed up at that time, I'm not sure I would have accepted it.

My public achievements in using my legal and humanitarian skills to help vulnerable people who have got into debt, are to me nothing compared to the achievement of turning my life around in my late 20s. This, though I say it myself, took courage and determination. I had shriveled as a human being. I had to rebuild myself, which once I had rediscovered my direction in life, was a step-by-step process, and eventually became enjoyable.

As you may know, my difficulties began in my early 20s when I found it hard to let go the wish to preserve my parents' marriage in aspic. Things change—even parents change—but I found it hard to accept this for a long time. So my first piece of advice is to accept situations that you cannot possibly alter—especially other people's relationships—and make the very best you can of them.

I compounded the mistake by turning in on myself, and resisting all attempts from my parents or their new partners to prize open my defensiveness. I even carried my hurt into my student life, and subsequently my work life. For several years I worked in a soulless job, working absurdly long hours, partly because the type of work demanded it, and partly to give myself no time to think.

Once I managed to get a grip on my priorities and my values—another recommendation to you as a life lesson—my life changed around. I began to work in a job that enabled me to help other people, and in doing so, help my self. Initially I worked in the field of debt in the developing world, but found a similar, urgent need on my doorstep. Credit card debt had been ballooning in this country. People were encouraged to buy things they could never pay for, and borrow money they could never repay. Worse, for the most part, the moneylenders—the credit card companies and so on—were levying exorbitant charges on them while they tried to sort it out. The Citizens Advice Bureaus had been doing an excellent job, but had been overwhelmed.

I was able to use my legal training both to help individuals and, eventually, with government support, to help change the rules of the game. The charity I helped set up—which both spoke on behalf of people who had had their vulnerability exploited by moneylenders in many guises, and acted on their behalf—has now become a model copied throughout the world.

The lesson that comes out of this, which might be helpful to you, is not that helping people in need is good. We know that. The significant lesson I took from the whole event was that if I had not been through the long dark night of the soul first, probably none of this would have happened. If I had not suffered extended pain from my parents' divorce, and gone through the refusal to let it go, I would probably have got some job that was worthwhile, but not difference-making in the sense that the charity has been.

The charity would never have happened, and many people who are living good lives today would have still been blighted by debt, with all its crushing, dehumanizing side-effects.

Not that I'm wishing a long dark night of the soul on you. Far from it. What I'm saying is that if one happens, good may come from it, and it's important to look positively for that good, in case you miss it.

My last piece of advice to you is to stay close to your family and friends, no matter what. I lost touch with my family over a number of years and it caused them, and me, much needless pain and heartache. I let too many friendships wither too, and it took a long time to rebuild them. I did so, and friends and family became—and are—central to my life. Avoid that mistake at all costs.

I hope this helps. It has certainly helped me putting it down on paper.

Have a fulfilling and happy life,

Your doting godmother,

Helen

Helen worried slightly that she seemed to be tempting fate by writing the letter as if there was an immediate happy ending. She knew there would be many obstacles on the way, but felt a growing sense of determination to overcome them.

So both Helen and Lee had begun to perceive things in their lives that had been far from clear before. Their insights had not yet given them a crystallized purpose, but they certainly had one or two important threads that could lead on to purpose. They had set out on their journeys of personal discovery and fulfillment.

If you have not yet written your obituaries and letter, now might be an appropriate to sit down to the task. If your spirit doesn't move you, make sure you move your spirit.

8

The Difference Imperative: choosing domains and making it happen

Now that you—along with Lee and Helen—are groping your way towards a clear articulation of your purpose, it's time to get down to particulars. It is very probable that the first attempt to define your purpose will not be your last. You may be lucky, and discover it in one attempt, with no further additions or deletions. For most of us, refinement is ongoing, as new stimuli occur in our lives to channel our compassion in new directions.

DIFFERING SHAPES AND SIZES OF PURPOSE

The reason for this flexibility is that we are likely to define our purpose slightly differently, according to what is going on in our lives at the moment we are addressing its definition. As a result, the ambitiousness and scope of our purposes will vary considerably. Remember, there is no single right answer, or one correct way of defining purpose.

Some examples will indicate the possible differences in scope between different people's definition of their purpose:

To help others to learn
To help others to eat
To help others to write
To help others to read
To help others learn to fish
To bring laughter into people's lives
To take my sport to a new level
To build a new business paradigm combining profit with compassion
To save young boys and girls from sexual exploitation
To paint pictures which move people
To touch people's hearts through song
To pioneer a new category of bio science
To be a great surgeon to save and improve lives
To nurse people with compassion and joy
To give my dying partner the happiest and most fulfilling last months possible
To get traffic flows changed at a local accident black spot

To help ex-prisoners live happy and useful lives back in society
To give my children the best possible start.

All these are worthwhile purposes, but they vary hugely in scope and ambition. **This in no way denigrates those with a smaller scope.** All it says is that we will all choose slightly different ways to create value, and make a difference.

BENEFICIAL PRESENCES

Many of the purposes stated above are the purposes of people who, at heart, are Beneficial Presences. Beneficial Presences have kind hearts and daily, in the words of Wordsworth, the great Romantic poet, do countless "little, nameless, unremembered acts of kindness and of love."

So someone with the purpose of bringing laughter into people's lives, or nursing patients with compassion and joy, or giving a dying partner the happiest and most fulfilling last months possible, is making a difference by being a Beneficial Presence. This probably includes such purposes as giving your children the best possible start. The difference to those children is great, but it is essentially brought about by the work of one person (possibly with their partner) making a big difference to a small number of people.

I would include teachers in Beneficial Presences. I was lucky enough to have several excellent teachers at school, but one, by the name of Bill Euston, stood out. Bill was a teacher of English Literature, and with him, the subject sang the most wonderful tunes for us pupils. He could make the driest of texts live with vibrancy and laughter. Even the essays of Francis Bacon (1561–1626) came alive with relevance, color, entertainment, and truth.

He would get so excited during lessons reading out texts that he would spit all over the front row of desks in his delight in what he was reading. There was great competition not to sit in the front row as a result. We always said we would take umbrellas into the classroom, and put them up when he started spitting, but we never did. He was a teacher of genius, and like many great teachers, preferred to teach lower-stream pupils more than the brighter students, because he felt he got more satisfaction from turning on the light for a dimmer student than a brighter one who would probably have got there anyway.

Bill Euston made a huge difference to my life. Like many of his students, I went on to study English Literature at university, and have loved it ever since. But Bill, by my definition, was a huge Beneficial Presence, rather than a Difference Driver or a Difference Deliverer. He transformed his pupils' appreciation of literature, and in so doing made a difference to their lives, but didn't attempt to change the status quo.

As a teacher (like nurses or doctors) he enhanced the status quo, utilizing huge talent, generosity, and humanity to do so. Of course some Difference Drivers—like Plato or Gandhi—use teaching as part of their means of transforming our perception of society. However, the scope of their goals—which are to transform, rather than to communicate—and the impact of their teaching, takes them beyond Beneficial Presences.

BENEFICIAL PRESENCES AND INFLICTED PURPOSE

Beneficial Presences are probably the most numerous of all difference makers, and for those they benefit, the most important. The Difference Drivers and Deliverers may get the headlines, but Beneficial Presences get the profound gratitude (sadly not always articulated) of those who are directly helped by their presence.

Because it is the nature of Beneficial Presences to rise to the occasion when a sudden crisis demands altruistic action—like the illness of a loved one—sometimes their purpose is inflicted upon them. They may not have chosen to be a Beneficial Presence to anyone, but suddenly a friend in difficulty, the death of a parent leaving the other parent desolate, or a colleague with an emotional crisis, catapults them into the opportunity, or the need, to serve.

If it is the opportunity to serve, it will be a voluntary act, and is likely to be roughly in line with our purpose, in the sense that it is a natural, spontaneous act of sympathy or compassion to be of assistance. The trigger to action resonates with our central purpose to serve others in need (whether defined or not), and can be responded to with generosity of spirit.

The trouble comes when the sudden crisis demanding our compassion does not instantly gel with our natural instincts (or lack of them) to serve. In fact the situation we find ourselves in is inconvenient, even oppressive. We didn't ask to be a Beneficial Presence, but the illness, absence, or even death of someone suddenly leaves us as the only person available to help. We'd rather be somewhere else, but the situation is clearly demanding that we rise to the occasion.

We then have four choices. Three are weak, but human and understandable. The fourth is difficult, very difficult, but the right one. The first alternative is to do nothing, and walk away from the situation. The second is to step up to the mark, but to hate and resent every moment of it, and let others know this is how you feel. The third is to respond to a code of duty for public purposes, but in private to be mean-spirited to the individual or individuals needing compassion or help.

The first three choices do not qualify the person making them for the title of Beneficial Presence. They may or may not be present, and they may or may not be beneficial, but they are not a difference maker in the sense of being wholehearted in their commitment to positively changing things for the better.

The fourth choice—the right one—is the decision to become what might be called an apprentice Beneficial Presence. This choice is to acknowledge that the situation is not of our choosing, is extremely inconvenient, but is there as a challenge to our humanity. We must rise to the occasion, and transform our initially resentful response into a wholehearted and generous one.

For most of us, to respond to the situation with warmth, love, and generosity, needs a deal of hard work. When circumstances inflict our purpose upon us, we must learn, step by step, to grow into a positive acceptance of it.

Once more it is back to character and courage. If the spirit doesn't move us, we must sit down and move our spirit. A positive act of will is required to move our response from meanness and resentment to wholehearted and positive acceptance of the opportunity fate has thrown at us to demonstrate our humanity. Our apprenticeship may be short or long, but in serving it with persistence and good humor, we will graduate over time to become a Beneficial Presence, which at times can be the highest form of courage.

BENEFICIAL PRESENCES, AND EXPLOITATION BY POISONERS AND TIME SPONGES

Whether you are a natural Beneficial Presence, or someone who has graduated to being one after a long and difficult apprenticeship, you will still need discipline to ensure you are not exploited. This is because certain types of people seek out Beneficial Presences to share what is in essence their own self-pity, or self-absorption. They sense a sympathetic ear, and make sure they get more than their fair share of it.

I am talking here mainly of the poisoners and the time sponges, not normal people who naturally want to share the warmth and humanity of Beneficial Presences. Poisoners are the negative, usually pessimistic, people who delight in trying to infect others with their sense of resentment of everything positive or life enhancing. They sap the energy of everyone they meet, and delight in spreading their negative, poisonous view of life.

They delight in spreading gossip, especially gossip that reflects badly on people they know, or envy. Negative gossip is pernicious, and will be avoided by people wanting to make a positive difference. Negative gossip damages at least three people, as soon as it is spoken. It damages the person being vilified by the gossiper. It damages the person receiving the gossip, because he/she is hearing another person being defamed who has been given no opportunity to defend him or herself. And it reduces the gossiper, because he/she is unfairly speaking badly of someone, often using unverified or second-hand information.

On the other hand, speaking well of someone enhances at least the same three people. The person praised behind his/her back is enhanced. The listener is enhanced to hear good of another human being, and the speaker is enhanced as he/she is seen as positive, and uplifting.

The 24-hour challenge

If you are serious about becoming a difference maker, and being trustworthy, then not spreading negative gossip is impor-tant. If you find the spreading of negative gossip too tempting to resist, it may be worth trying the following exercise. For the next 24 hours, try speaking only well of people. If you find yourself spreading gossip, or speaking ill of people, start the 24 hours again. Then move up to a week, and so on, until the need and desire to spread gossip is a distant memory, as you find the uplift of saying good things about people more enjoyable and rewarding.

Poisoners revel in negative gossip, and love putting people down. They love subverting positive situations and positive people. Their weapons are half-truths, rumors, and the manip-ulation of facts to their own twisted perspective. For you, it may be a colleague who is a poisoner, or it may even be a relative. Whoever it is, if you are serious about being a Beneficial Pres-ence to someone (not the poisoner), to be able to operate effec-tively you will need to neutralize his or her toxicity,

To do this there are two choices. One is to confront poison-ers, and say words to the effect that their behavior is causing you distress, and if they don't change you will have to take steps to reduce their presence in your life, otherwise you will be dragged down by them. Alternatively, actually avoid as much contact as is possible with them. This may cause pain, but in the long run, if you allow their poisonous presence to continue, you will not only be unhappy but unable to be productive as a difference maker, because your positive energy will have been neutered by their destructive behavior. The tough truth is that it is almost impossible to be a Beneficial Presence to a poisoner. It can be done, but it requires huge courage and commitment on your part, to avoid being taken down with them.

Time sponges are very different from poisoners. They are not intentionally unpleasant or damaging, they just grab any available ear to pour out their concerns or their troubles. They seem to live in a personal time-free zone. They appear to have nothing important to do (apart from talk about themselves), and therefore assume nobody else has either.

They drift through life, often late for everything, allowing others to sweep up the mess, and sort things out for them. They cannot understand why people (especially parents) get frustrated at their inability to connect in any efficient way with the world.

This in itself would be all right if they didn't suck in the time of anyone patient or loving enough to enter their world of timelessness. They absorb acres of other people's time, without any insight into their sponge-like activities. Unlike poisoners, time sponges often benefit from the presence of Beneficial Presences. This is because they are often good and deserving people, but, for some reason, not plugged in to those surrounding them in an insightful or sympathetic way. Some become more insightful and sympathetic over time, but they need to be dealt with on an ongoing basis, whether they are evolving or not. The solution is not easy, as it throws up the apparently antithetical concepts of human feelings and efficiency.

The essence of the challenge is to bring time efficiency to a relationship with a self-absorbed soul wanting to take up time in a totally inefficient way (either talking, or having his or her life organized). It's not easy, but it is possible—and necessary if the difference we want to make as a Beneficial Presence is to bring some disciplines into the life of a time sponge.

The first priority is to make a better job of protecting your own time. Time management books can be very helpful in helping us achieve this. They remind us how inefficient we are at organizing our time, and give very useful pointers. Just as we might have set times at work when we deal with emails or phone calls, and leave the rest of the day free for other types of work, we might have set times during the day or evening when the time is our time, not to be invaded by time sponges.

It is important to create something that works for you, explain it fully to the time sponge, and then stick to it with discipline and determination, especially in the early stages, when it will be challenged by the person who is losing unrestricted access to you.

The next stage will be to try to introduce some of these time management disciplines to the time sponges. Remember confrontation can be a loving act. It will be extremely challenging to start with, but eventually, they may come to thank you for it. If they do, you will have made a profound difference for them.

CHOOSING OUR DOMAIN

Whether we intend to become a Beneficial Presence, a Difference Driver, or a Difference Deliverer, we come now to the formal disciplines of the Make a Difference Mindset. The first step is to establish the domain we intend to operate in. This may be self-evident from our purpose, but it is important to confirm where the majority of our efforts to make a difference will be centered.

It is possible to make a difference in more than one domain at a time. You may be making a significant difference at work, while at the same time bringing about an improvement in a difficult child at home. Generally speaking, most of us do not have the energy, or the mental resources, to change the world in more than one domain at a time.

We are not precluded, therefore, from being a Difference Driver in one domain, while being a Beneficial Presence in other domains. The reason for the need to focus is that most human beings can't have more than one major idea in their head at the same time.

Many years ago I worked in an advertising agency. Often clients asked to put too much information in the advertisements. One of my colleagues had a simple way of demonstrating that one benefit was all most consumers could concentrate on at a time. He would pick up a couple of sugar lumps, and say to the client, "Catch these!" The client would look at both sugar lumps flying through the air, and inevitably drop both. "There," he would say, "That's what advertising is like. If I throw one idea, people will catch it. If I throw two, they'll drop both."

It's a bit like that with making a difference. Have one clear difference you want to make, and you may achieve it. Have several, and you're likely to lose them all in the quicksand. So our first decision is in what domain will I make a difference? Here are some choices:

Artistic—will it involve my life as a painter/musician/dancer/ photographer/engraver/collector/writer/producer?

Work—will it involve my work as a director/manager/worker/ trade unionist?

Home/Family—will it involve my wife/husband/partner/child/ parents/relatives/ step-relatives?

Spiritual—will it involve my meditation/religion/personal god?

Social—will it involve volunteering/community work/social service?

Sport/Games—will it involve my performance, or my support for my sport, my game?

Physical health—will I be seeking to improve/transform my health?

Mental health—will it involve a healthier lifestyle/personal development/escape from toxic friends?

The choice is wide, bringing with it the need for focus. This applies whatever domain you choose. If you choose the domain of sport, music, art, or whatever, you will need to make up your mind whether your purpose takes towards being a Beneficial

Presence (in which case you will probably be a team player rather than a solo performer who makes a difference—on the field of sport, in the orchestra, or part of an art movement).

If on the other hand you decide to become a Difference Driver, moving the standards of your domain on to new levels, you will need to decide what sort of a solo star you intend to be. Once you've selected your domain, are you going to become tomorrow's version of Pele, the Beatles, or Picasso?

Once we are clear on our domain, and our role within that domain, we can move on to the consideration of our Difference Imperative.

THE DIFFERENCE IMPERATIVE

The Difference Imperative is what drives us to act, and to do the things necessary to create value, which in turn causes a difference to be made. The Difference Imperative is the conjunction of our purpose (which may be sufficient on its own), our stimulus to act (the importance and urgency to us of the difference we have decided on), and finally the quality of the concept we decide on to make a difference.

So there are three forces at work. The first is our purpose, and the passion it engenders in us to create new value. The second is the power of the stimulus (such as the death of a near relative), and the third is the concept we decide on (such as a charity in their name for sufferers of the disease which killed them). This third force builds into a fourth step, which is to brand the concept, so it is motivating, and quickly understood and communicated.

The second, third, and fourth elements are just as crucial as the first to make significant differences happen. A generalized desire to make a difference that does not have a specific and motivating outcome is doomed to struggle. It is very unlikely ever to happen.

Let's take two examples. A powerful stimulus like defenseless innocent prisoners being tortured precipitates the concept of a charity funding lawyers to defend those prisoners and highlight abuses. This finally is given energy and definition by *branding* it with a name that becomes memorable and engaging— Amnesty International.

Then again, extreme poverty on the doorstep of Muhammad Yunus was the *stimulus* that sparked a specific and powerful *concept*—micro loans. This in term evolved into the *brand* of the Grameen Bank. The combination of elements can have enormous impact in helping the difference to happen, because it excites minds, stimulates compassion, and creates energy.

REFINING THE STIMULUS TO ENHANCE THE COMMITMENT

As we have seen with the Grameen Bank it is possible for the stimulus to reveal the purpose. The purpose needs to be there; otherwise the stimulus will fall on stony ground, and will not flower. It may, however, be helpful to heighten the stimulus to bring the purpose into focus.

If, say, you feel your purpose is to help the starving, it may be helpful to research different areas of famine or undernourishment, to find one that especially engages your compassion. Research it on the Internet, talk to aid workers at the charities involved, even make a trip to one or two areas yourself. Seeing individuals suffering at first, or even second, hand makes a huge difference to motivation.

The fundraising events staged by some television channels are often supercharged by the celebrities involved going out and experiencing the situation in person. It is apparent that they are visibly moved by what they are seeing. Their commitment moves from the brain to the heart, and it makes their ability to appeal for funds to help remedy the situation much more powerful as a result.

Your personal stimulus may be so strong that you have no need to work on it in any way. But if this is not the case, everything you can do to engage with the stimulus will enhance your commitment, and thus your ability to deliver a worthwhile difference.

If at any time you find your courage under pressure, and your motivation flagging, going back to your stimulus can be reinvigorating. Revisiting your stimulus on a regular basis is always worthwhile. It reminds you why you are striving to create value to bring about a positive difference, and it provides fresh energy.

Most domains have a powerful ability to provide an inspiring stimulus. In sport, for example, there are countless examples of young runners, or football players, who have had strong purpose (passion for their sport) but have been inspired by a great specific performance of one of their heroes or heroines to redouble their efforts to become great players or champions themselves. The Olympic Games, each time it takes place, inspires the next generation of athletes and sportsmen and women to become tomorrow's champions.

So we now have our purpose, and we either have, or are working on having, our stimulus. Next we come to nailing our concept to make a difference.

CHOOSING THE CONCEPT THAT WILL MAKE THE DIFFERENCE

This can be extremely challenging. Sometimes the solution is simple—establish a charity to help other people with the disease that killed our loved one, or form a committee to prevent heavy lorries from coming through our housing estate—but quite often the best way of making a difference is not so obvious.

If you work for an organization which has a worthwhile purpose, but is feebly led, and falling down on the job of providing the benefits it should be providing, what is your concept to change things for the better? If you want to make a difference to your family's diet, and your attempts to improve it are foiled by impenetrable food labeling that prevents you discovering its provenance or suitability—what is your concept to make the difference you seek?

So some concepts need some pretty profound reflection, coupled with some imagination, to deliver a workable answer. There is no short cut. The quality of the input (the concept you come up with) will equal the quality of the output (how effective the concept is in changing things for the better). When searching for a concept powerful enough to be able to create sufficient new value to change things, be as imaginative and radical as you can be. Daring ideas excite people and change situations.

BRANDING THE CONCEPT

This may sound somewhat superficial, and not in keeping with the high dignity of making a difference. Forget it. We live in a world increasingly dominated by brands—from countries, to products and services, to universities, right through to charities—they are now all brands. The value of brands such as Amnesty International or Médecins Sans Frontières—and many, many others—is absolutely massive.

Although Naomi Klein, in her book *No Logo*, did some useful work in exposing some unacceptable abuses, she completely missed the point that brands are of inestimable value to all of us. In a confusing and complicated world, they are a shorthand way of communicating the value of something.

Once we have a brand to consider—whether it's a chocolate bar or a charity—we know its depth and width, its personality, its trustworthiness. It saves an enormous amount of time researching the product or service—its brand name supplies much of the information we need.

It is important to recognize that a brand's true franchise exists in the minds of its consumers, as well as the wider audience that may not consume it, but have views on it. Whatever brand owners may say, or claim, it is the experience of consumers that is judge and jury as to whether a brand is trusted, or rejected.

As brands are built on trust, and trust alone, they have to deliver, or they will wither and die. What makes a brand stand out is the value it creates for its consumers. This is its core value proposition. This may be the added benefits it supplies, or it may be a stunningly low price. Ikea, the furniture store, and one or two of the low-priced airlines, are strong brands because they have a value proposition that sets them apart from commodity products.

This, indeed, is the origin of the word "brand." Cattle were branded—with a red-hot branding iron—to distinguish them from the cattle from another farm or ranch. In the Industrial Revolution, towns and cities began to get more populous, trains instead of horses and carts began to carry produce, so products arrived at markets from further and further afield. Some way of identifying the provenance of products like butter or cheese, and subsequently products like soap, was needed. A stamp—to show the farm or factory or origin—was the brand that distinguished a product of which the producer was proud, from products that were commodities, and came from nobody knew where.

So people came to trust brands, because they had a good idea where they came from, and knew where to go to complain, if they were not up to scratch. Brands have come a long way since then, of course, but the essence—distinguishing one brand from another, and from commodity alternatives—is down to the ability of the brand to create a reputation for **its distinctive core value.**

So if we are serious about making a difference, we may need to brand our concept. It is important to understand this in no way diminishes the importance of a clear and compelling concept. The solution to the situation we want changed needs to be workable, and—ultimately—achievable. As with all brands, the quality of the content and its consistency and efficacy— whether it's a product or a service—is what gives it longevity and earns it trust.

There are a lot of people out there trying to make a difference, and that's commendable. If we want to make a real difference, which demands we make waves, then we need both a powerful concept and a branding of it that will come over time to be recognized. The brand reputation will not happen overnight. It is the nature of brands to be tested by the marketplace before they are accepted.

As we will see later—especially with Lee—the branding of the concept has two benefits. The first benefit is that the disciplines necessary to define the essence of the brand mean that the offer has to be refined and clarified with great care. The second benefit is that other people can understand what the new value of the difference they are making is made up of, and whether they find it relevant and motivating.

Generally speaking, it is the Difference Drivers who create and launch the brand. Difference Deliverers examine the new brand, see that it accords with their purpose and stimulus, become part of the brand, and in doing so, become crucial to making it a success. Difference Deliverers are vital to brand building. It is they who make it happen. Grameen Bank's 14,000 employees are all both brand builders and brand ambassadors. The doctors and nurses working for Médecins Sans Frontières, too, are brand builders and ambassadors.

When we volunteer to work for a well-known charity we are thus becoming part of that brand, and helping to keep it fresh in the minds of potential donors. We are Difference Deliverers, helping to sustain the value created by the brand to help the cause we are supporting, either by direct action, or by money.

Whether we are Drivers or Deliverers, once we have worked through the stages of our Difference Imperative, we need to set about establishing some specific goals, and some measurable outputs.

GOAL SETTING: IMPORTANT, BUT DON'T GET TOO HUNG UP ON IT

Now we come to making our plan to start putting our Make a Difference Mindset into practice, we must look at goals as another important stimulus to action. There is a lot of information out there on goal setting. There are lots of books on the subject, and many of them are excellent. I must confess, however, that from time to time I have felt I was overdosing on goals. The reason is that during various parts of my life when I have set lots of goals, I failed to reach most of them.

The reason was, I suspect, that they were generally associated with areas of my life that I either didn't have that much control over, or weren't, deep down, that important to me. In the early 1990s I had a business go from more than a decade of great success to a period of huge financial challenge. The causes were a combination of economic pressures, increased competition, lack of liquidity, and changes in the market.

We had to sell the business, and I had to start again. The company had been worth millions, but by the time we sold, it was worth very little. With none of the wealth I had expected to materialize from the company, I had to begin a new life, at the same time as supporting a young and growing family. I kept setting financial goals for my income, and I kept missing them. After much frustration, and three of four years of slightly straitened financial circumstances, I came to realize that actually I was more interested in what I was doing each working day (I had the privilege of working from home amongst the creative chaos created by a busy wife and lively children) than I was in earning a huge income.

I therefore began to set far fewer goals, and began to center them on specific tasks, which I could deliver on, rather than on income levels which I couldn't really control, or didn't have a deep emotional commitment to. I do not, however, underestimate the power of goals. An event that brought this home to me took place in the summer of 1986, when we were on holiday in south-west France.

One morning I went for a run, both to start to get back in shape, and in order to feel virtuous for the rest of the day. The house we were staying in was at the top of a very large hill, so the only way I could run was down. I finally arrived at the village at the foot of the hill, and turned round to start the long climb home. It was hard work from the start, and became no easier as I got into the climb. By two-thirds of the way up I was in trouble. I was running at the slowest pace you could run, and still call it running, rather than walking.

I couldn't see the top of the hill, as it was obscured by the twists and turns of the road, and a dense undergrowth of trees and bushes. Having little idea of the progress I was making, I started to set myself targets, to break it down to bite-sized chunks—this next bush, that next tree. It eventually got so uncomfortable that I knew I wasn't going to make it. I therefore set myself a final target of a wooden post carrying a power line about 100 meters further up the hill. It was getting nearer, but painfully slowly, as my legs felt like lead, and my lungs heaved with the effort.

It was so difficult, that for the last 15 yards I had to shut my eyes in a feeble attempt to shut out the pain. I opened them again, hoping desperately that I had made it, and I could stop. The pole was still about 3 meters away, but as I saw it, I also saw the brim of the hill, about 150 meters further on.

Somehow, I discovered new energy, and kept going to the top. As I flopped into a deckchair when I got back to the house, I reflected that if someone had told me that I would have made the top at any time before I actually saw it, I would not have believed him or her. I was completely drained—the heat and the hill had defeated me. Seeing my goal of the top of the hill somehow drove new strength to my legs and new oxygen to my lungs, and I made it.

As we start out on our journey to confirm our purpose, it may, or may not, be that goals are relevant. I suspect that Muhammad Yunus, when he was in the early stages of finding a solution to the grinding poverty of some of his compatriots in Bangladesh, did not set too many goals. He just wanted to find a solution, and make it happen. As the project evolved, and the Grameen Bank began to understand the potential in the market, and its ability to emancipate and empower people to create and sustain their own enterprises, it probably began to set specific goals.

Once you get to critical mass, as the bank did, you then certainly need both goals and controls. If, as Grameen have done, you intend to bring mobile telephony on a call-by-call basis to villages in Bangladesh, you need to know how many mobile phones to negotiate with the suppliers, and as the loan portfolio grows, you need to know how much capital you require to raise to meet projected demand. But for people in the very early stages of creating value, and making a difference, getting hung up on goals can be counter-productive.

If, however, you are blessed with an overpowering sense of purpose, and you know clearly how you are going to change the world, do go for big goals. In business they are called GBHG— Great Big Hairy Goals. These are stretch goals that excite the imagination by showing things can be changed by large amounts, not just incremental amounts. If such goals feel right for you—go for them.

If this isn't the case, set very few goals, and make them achievable. Make them specific to tasks, and put a date on them, so you are answerable to yourself for accomplishing them by a specific time.

If you don't feel goals are relevant—you know your purpose, you have a stimulus, you have worked out your concept, and it seems appropriate to make it a brand—forget the goals. Just get on with it, and make it happen. Indeed, make making it happen your goal.

Most successful business case histories are written after the event, with the benefit of hindsight. They are presented in a way that makes the story look as if it were all tidy and premeditated. Life is never like that. Feel free to have specific goals if you feel they will help, but if you don't, make it happen anyway. You can always write the goals in later, when you are successful, and you are presenting your personal case history of how you created great value, and made a huge difference.

The one stipulation I would make is that you put a date on making it happen. It is all very well to operate in a goal-free zone while we are in the creative frenzy of creating some new, relevant value for other human beings, or setting new standards or ground-rules in the domain we have chosen to operate in. But if we put no date on it we cease to be answerable either to ourselves, or to the people we are trying to help, or to the new standards we are trying to achieve.

If however, we have a date and a definition, however loose, of the difference we are aiming to make, we then have a plan for which we are responsible. We have defined the output we are aiming for, and the time period over which that output will be delivered. We may fail to deliver, but vagueness and wriggle room for non-action is removed.

So settle on a date, write it down, and put it in places where you will see it. Stick it on the wall by your bed, write it on the back of your hand, and put it on your computer as a screen saver. Make sure you see it several times a day.

Doing this, we'll become accountable to ourselves for making significant efforts to make a difference. When the going gets tough, and purpose and stimulus dwindle, a combination of courage and accountability will get us through. Of course we need to have built character for accountability to be meaningful.

Once again, character and purpose are confirmed as the origins of the enduring ability to deliver on making a difference. Being captains of our souls makes the difference in making a difference.

9

The Difference Imperative

Lee and Helen find their purpose, refine their stimulus, develop their concept, and start to brand it

LEE FIGHTS THE GOOD FIGHT

Remembering P, the operations director's words, "We're an endangered species, Lee, but we can't give up the good fight!" Lee determined to follow the advice.

As far as he was concerned, the fight was for the soul of the company, and that was worth fighting for. He had worked for the organization for over eight years, and had put a lot of heart into helping it to grow and be successful. He felt saddened and frustrated at its current lack of direction, and over-narrow focus on the financial bottom line.

Reflecting on the loss of direction, Lee realized that the changes of ownership, coupled with the current CEO being cost-obsessed, had brought about a severe dilution of the company's brand equity. What had previously been a strong brand, with clear values and a strong reputation, had drifted over recent years into becoming a commodity, rather than a brand. Most of its advertising focused on price offers, with what the company stood for being taken for granted.

Strong brands are extremely resilient. They can take a surprising amount of abuse and neglect from their owners before they wither and die. Most strong brands can be resuscitated and brought back to rude health, even after the market has written them off. Consumers have long memories, and are prepared to forgive, as long as the brand comes back with similar strong values and seeks to rebuild its lost reputation.

The brand's original values had been clear, and had resonated with Lee, which was one of the main reasons he joined the company. The brand stood for openness and honesty in a market that at that time was a roaring commodity market, with the phones and services being sold on price. But this was a commodity market with a difference. The major operators all practiced confusion marketing, which meant they published impenetrable tariffs with great-sounding deals, which couldn't be compared with other networks because there were no common points of comparison.

Lee's firm had cut through all this, genuinely taking the customer's side. The taking of sides was genuine, because it was one of the pioneers of what came to be called the "internal brand". The internal brand is the brand perception of those who really know what is going on—the employees and the suppliers. Sometimes this can be out of kilter with what the advertising and marketing is saying about the brand. In Lee's company's case, the internal and the external brand sang the same song.

The core value of the company—which it lived up to—was to create as much value as possible for the customer. This sounds obvious, but in fact was the reverse of what the company's competitors in the market were doing. Lee's company strove to give value, while the competition sought to take value. Their competitors' focus was to screw as much revenue as possible from their customers, whereas Lee's company's focus was to create the best possible service, for a fair return.

Each time the company introduced a new benefit on the service—and it pioneered several innovations that the rest of the industry adopted—the company charged a fair price for it (or no price increase at all, if it cost the company nothing), rather than following the industry practice of charging an unjustified premium rate for it until competitors copying it forced the price down.

The company's tariff was clear, and easy to understand. It didn't charge for every conceivable extra. There were no expensive premium rates kicking in at unexpected moments. The staff lived the brand, and thought of themselves as customers, so nothing was done to take advantage of, or upset, their outside customers.

Lee reveled in this open, honest, enthusiastic, culture. What was particularly satisfying was that customers liked the brand's values too. They stayed longer (customer churn—encouraged by commodity marketing—was very high in the industry, but much lower for his company), and they spent more money (they felt they could use their phones more, because they would be charged a fair rate, rather than being ripped off). This meant the company, as it grew, was more highly valued by the stock exchange, and more profitable than its competitors.

The downside of this success was that the company attracted predators, and was bought and sold several times to take out value for shareholders. The resulting decline in share price contained many factors, but one of them was that the previous high rating was partly based on its better than average customer retention, and higher than average spend per customer, earned by the values of fairness and openness. Both these key indicators were now below the average for the industry.

So Lee's company had a mountain to climb. He realized his major priority was to address the challenge of culture decline. The culture had once been uplifting, giving employees a sense of meaning, but was now rapidly becoming toxic. There were no common goals, no common purpose, and no sense of teamwork. Only a few lone voices, like Lee, and the operations director P, still felt the situation could be reversed, and it was worth the effort involved to do so.

Lee realized he was taking on a big challenge. This was in the area of Difference Driving, rather than Difference Delivery, so great were the forces ranked against him. He decided to take it step by step. The following weekend, after the kids were in bed, he went off to his small den in the back of the house. He opened up his laptop, called up the folder with his letter and obituaries in and opened a new file, with the title **Purpose**.

To start himself off he typed, **"Fight the good fight."** He thought for a long time about the issues involved (as he had been for some weeks now), and finally made a stab at his purpose. He typed:

> **To improve the culture of the company, and the openness of its communications.**

He thought about it, and realized that, while it was a fair reflection of what he wanted to do, it was too vague. Its woolliness left too many escape routes for failing to deliver on his purpose. He needed to define it more accurately, so there was clarity about what his purpose specifically was.

He tried again:

To recreate the company's values of fairness and concern for customers.

Again, it was true, but what concerned him was that it didn't get to the heart of what he saw as the company's sickness. His purpose, he was coming to realize, was to transform the fundamental integrity of the company. He could see lip service being paid to values like fairness and concern for customers—who could disagree that they were desirable values to have? This lip service might not then translate into the radical culture change Lee saw as crucial to the company once more having an internal and external brand that was totally aligned. Unless the values were lived, rather than talked about, it wouldn't stick.

Finally, he got to something closer to what he felt his purpose to be. He knew he might refine it as time went on, but it seemed to get to the heart of his concerns for the company's continued health, as a successful supplier of goods and services, and as a worthwhile place to work. He wrote:

To improve radically the openness and honesty of behavior, and eliminate cynicism within the company.

He was slightly taken aback at the directness of his words. At the same time, he felt a sense of release. This was exactly the issue that touched his hot button. He was passionate about integrity and fairness, and couldn't stand the cynicism and backbiting, which was becoming more and more prevalent.

This was indeed his purpose. If he could get the company back to its positive and uplifting culture of honesty, fairness, and concern for customers, he would have made a huge difference. He would have created value for himself, the other employees, and the customers. And as a result, for the shareholders.

Lee went on to think about the **stimulus** that he could draw on to motivate himself to keep going when challenges and obstacles were thrown in his path. This, for Lee, was relatively straightforward. It was based on the powerful motivation of fear that took the form of his intense concern about the decline of the company he still loved. He wrote:

> **Preventing the impending victory for cynicism, and the implosion of positive values, with all the ensuing fall-out.**

This seemed to him to get to the nub of the matter. As far as Lee was concerned, he was fighting to save both the company, and his own and many other people's jobs. It was a battle worth engaging in.

Lee had read widely in business literature on culture change, and a book that had especially impressed him was *Good to Great*, by Jim Collins (the co-author, with Jerry Porras, of *Built to Last*). The book describes a small group of companies moving from good to exceptional performance, and examines the common themes in their success. Two conclusions emerged from all the evidence compiled by the researchers that seemed relevant to the situation in Lee's company.

The first was that culture change has to be driven from the top, but that this does not require a charismatic chief executive to bring it about. On the contrary, the successful case histories indicated that long-serving, quiet but tough insiders brought about change more effectively than big-shot CEOs hired in to fix things. Lee's CEO qualified on two counts. First, he wasn't remotely charismatic, and second, he had been with the company for some time before being made CEO, so could be counted as an insider. (Unfortunately, he had been a rather soulless financial director before his promotion, and had concentrated on the numbers, not being very interested in the culture of the company.)

The second conclusion from the study described in the book was that it was vital to do what was described as getting the right people on the bus, getting them into the right position on the bus, and finally but importantly, getting the wrong people off the bus. In terms of getting people in the right position on the bus, Lee suspected his CEO was a better financial director than he was a CEO, but he couldn't do anything about that. What he could perhaps influence was getting the wrong people off the bus.

Lee was a kind and humane man, but recognized that one or two of what he called the poisoners were deeply cynical people, who would not change. These people would block and subvert any attempt to create a more positive culture. He knew change could not take place successfully with them still in the company. He felt it would be better for them (they might find a more amenable culture elsewhere), and the company, if they left.

This brought him on to the next stage of his Difference Imperative—his need for a **concept**, and a plan of campaign to enable him to fulfill his purpose. It was getting late, so he carried that endeavor over to the following day.

The night's sleep gave a chance for his subconscious to work on the problem, and he got up next morning with a plan almost fully formed. Lee's plan was simple. It was:

> **To put together the business case and delivery model for culture change, and present it to the CEO.**

This meant working out the financial benefits of reverting to a culture of fairness and value creation, so the CEO could see it wasn't some woolly soft-issues nonsense, but a bottom-line-oriented course of action. Coupled with this, a detailed plan for *how* the culture would be changed would also need to be worked out. Crucially, it wasn't just of getting the nod from the CEO. He had to buy into it both intellectually and emotionally, as he would be the key leader in the culture change.

Lee thought about it, and realized he would need help. His two strongest allies in the company were P, the operations director, and H, the human resources director. H and Lee had been great friends for many years. They shared the same aspirations, and same need for meaning in their work. If anything, H was even more frustrated than Lee at developments within the company.

He was frustrated for two reasons. First, it pained him to see the company's original values wither—despite his best efforts to sustain them. Second, as human resources director, his job function had changed radically over the past couple of years. In the formative years of the company the human resources department (or personnel department as it then was) had been located at the strategic core of the company. The original CEO, a man of vision, had realized that in an industry that was essentially a service industry—even though it sold phones and network connections—the quality of the employees would be of central importance. Those employees needed to be of high quality, highly trained, and highly motivated. A strong positive culture had to be created inside the company to make the brand work outside the company.

This meant that the human resources department was a creative function, and was as important as marketing or operations. Indeed all three roles overlapped, working together to make the brand happen.

Sadly, over recent years changes in company ownership, and the resulting loss of the founders' vision, had seen a dwindling in the role of HR. It no longer played a central, strategic role. It was banished to the outer darkness of the traditional HR functions of payroll, and hiring and firing at the behest of fairly junior line managers, who had little concern for culture, but a large concern for delivering this month's results.

So H had become more and more marginalized, and more and more frustrated. Like Lee, he felt the company's soul was worth fighting for, but had become increasingly gloomy on the prospects of success.

Over the following days, Lee managed to get a meeting together after work with P and H. He outlined his proposal, and both listened with interest. When he had finished, there was a pause. Eventually H broke the silence. "Mmm," he said, "You hit a few nails on the head there, Lee. It's an all-or-nothing plan. He either buys into it, or we are all dead men. The integrity issue is what it is all about. You can't avoid it. But if he sees it as a personal attack on him, we're history."

They both looked at P, who of all of them was the least dispensable to the organization, being a more than competent operations director, a key role for any company in their industry. He said quietly, "You are our conscience, Lee. And I thank you for that. The problem—as I'm sure you're both aware—is that the man we are dealing with is not very strong on the humanity stakes. He's a decent and well-meaning man, but he's a bean counter who's in his first CEO job, and may not have the confidence to back this plan. Frankly, I can't see him being able to get passionate about it, and it'll need passion to sell it to the shareholders. The financial benefits aren't immediate. It'll need faith and patience, to wait for them to come through."

Lee felt a cold feeling inside. The truth of the words struck him like a fist. He felt his courage ebbing away. He sat there for a few moments without speaking. He set about recalling his stimulus to bolster his courage:

> **Preventing the impending victory for cynicism, and the implosion of positive values, with all the ensuing fall-out.**

Yes, he thought, it is worth fighting for, even if, for me—and probably P and H—the fall-out may come sooner than intended.

"You're right," said Lee. "One thing's for sure. It won't be a walkover. But it's got to be worth a crack. If we don't try now, the situation will be irrecoverable, and we'll never forgive ourselves."

Both P and H sat silent for a while. Finally H broke the tension. "Damn and blast you, Lee. You're putting us on the spot. And you're right to do so. I'm up for it. My only regret is that it wasn't me that took the initiative. I'm HR, it should have been me that was embarrassing you blokes to come clean. Right. I'm off the fence. Let's go for it."

They both looked at P, who clearly was suffering some inner turmoil. Eventually P nodded. "OK," said. "I'm in. It won't be an easy sale, and we better have Plan B ready, if we fail. Plan A has to be the right option, though. Let's give it a go."

It was agreed that over the following weeks all three of them would meet up for a short session on a Friday evening, to work out the business case, and put together a plan to deliver the culture change, should their pitch to the CEO be successful. They also put out discreet soundings with headhunters, and were agreeably surprised at how much their services might be in demand, if Plan A blew up in their faces, and an alternative job might be required.

Lee and P did most of the work on the financial justification for the culture revamp, and H, as human resources director, put together the plan for bringing about the culture change within the company, should they gain the agreement of the chief executive. This involved values mapping of where the company had been, where it was now, and where it wanted to get to in the future. It also involved plans for investment in training for the desired culture, and humane exit routes for the cynics who resisted retraining.

Lee realized that both for the presentation to the CEO and the subsequent program to make it happen, he needed a **brand.** He needed it both for them to crystallize their thinking as to what their concept was, and for the chief executive to be able to grasp it more readily.

This did not turn out to be easy. Issues of culture are somewhat impalpable, and do not lend themselves to snappy definitions. After much thought, and many false starts, they came up with the branding of the concept.

The Virtuous Value Centrifuge

They appreciated this was not a brand name that instantly communicated the full concept, but had come to the conclusion that in the field of culture change and values definition it was unlikely that anything ever would. The central idea that the brand attempted to communicate was the move from a vicious circle of value degradation to a virtuous circle of value creation, which throws off value centrifugally as it turns.

A brand—any brand—can be said to be made up of three elements, all circling around the core of the brand. Those elements feed one into another. The elements are the **customer experience**—how the customer values and experiences the product or service; **communications** in the widest sense of all the consumer touch points—the advertising, promotion, phone answering, job application answering and so on; and the **quality of people and behavior** of the brand's employees. In service brands, like Lee and his colleagues', the latter element is particularly important.

The quality of staff and their behavior feed directly into the customer experience. If a customer sees an employee raise his eyes to the heavens to a colleague behind another customer's back, it is usually symptomatic of a lack of respect for customers in general. If employees are arrogant and contemptuous, rather than supportive and caring, this eats like a cancer into the customer's perception of the brand.

The circle of customer experience, communications, and quality of staff and their behavior is dynamic and interactive. It is either a vicious circle—negative experience at consumer touchpoints on each of the elements in the circle compound each other, leading to a decline in the brand's reputation amongst its consumers.

Or it is a virtuous circle—when good-quality staff are caring, fair and supportive to customers, create a positive customer experience, which is confirmed in the brand's communications, and results in an improving brand reputation. Customer appreciation in turn feeds back into employees finding their work more rewarding. Indeed, this gives it more meaning.

The centrifuge part of the brand name was an attempt to capture this—a sense of value being created and thrown off centrifugally, as the virtuous circle of value creation rotates.

Brands, like all things, are either growing or dying. A static state does not exist in nature, and it does not exist in business. It was Lee and his colleague's intention to communicate to the chief executive that their brand was in fact dying, even if the bottom line could be milked for a bit longer by stringent cost-cutting.

Hence the brand name of the Virtuous Value Centrifuge. Lee, using his engineer's training, produced some flow charts with excellent graphics to dramatize the brand, and its relevance of its message for the company. Value was shown being thrown off from the rotating brand for customers, employees, and shareholders.

Eventually the trio felt they were ready for the presentation to the CEO. A date was fixed at 9 o'clock on a Friday morning, some three weeks off. Lee reviewed his preparation. He felt that he was in reasonable shape on the character front—indeed he felt that in doing what he was doing he was showing evidence of his integrity and his captaincy over his soul. His courage was strong, but remembering the sinking feeling when P had come up with his disarmingly frank assessment of their chances of their success at their first meeting, Lee took the precaution of programming himself to be a Mighty Lion, should the occasion demand it.

In fact, the occasion did demand it. Lee, H and P had gone through their presentation the night before, and agreed to meet 15 minutes before the meeting, outside the CEO's office. Lee and H were there at the appointed hour, but there was no sign of P. They rang him on his mobile, but it was turned off. At 8.55, the CEO's door opened, and out came P, looking ashen faced.

He sat down with his two friends, and shook his head. "You won't believe this," he said. "There's been a reshuffle. I've just been made general manager for all territories overseas. I start next Monday. I just won't be around to help you guys."

He paused. Then continued, "Of course I'll carry on with the pitch, but I just won't be here to help you see the thing through if we get the go-ahead."

Lee felt his insides dissolving. For a few moments his brain seemed paralyzed, and he was unable to think. It was at this point he remembered his Mighty Lion anchor, which he had located on the bottom of his right ear lobe. He touched it, and, to his surprise, he felt his paralyzing state begin to turn into an enabling state.

"Nonsense," he said, "Ridiculous waste of time. You'll be in that meeting standing on one leg. Half your brain will be on your new job—congratulations by the way—and the other half will be hovering uncomfortably in the room with us. On your way, and good luck." He gently took P by the shoulder and ushered him towards the outer door.

Am I mad? he thought, as P disappeared. But he knew he had done the right thing. P had been given a significant promotion, and it would have been wrong to put it at risk, especially as P would be in a more powerful position for the future to influence events in other countries, and new territories, as they opened up. Also, having him in the meeting would have been a liability. It would have completely confused the CEO, and would have clouded the clarity of their message.

So Lee and H girded up their loins, and walked in to the CEO's office. In fact, the presentation went well, and they both felt they had explained their case as well as they could have hoped for. The CEO sat in silence throughout. At the end, he said, "Thank you gentlemen. Very interesting," stood up and shook their hands. "Do you have any questions?" asked Lee. "Not at this stage, no," answered the CEO, and ushered them from his office.

Lee and H had no clue as to what sort of impression they had created. They went back to their offices baffled about what the outcome might be to their initiative. The days passed, with still no response from the CEO. They asked to see him, but found he was too busy to fit them in.

Then flickers of response began to emerge. Not from the CEO, who remained silent and inscrutable. Instead, they came from senior colleagues who began to smirk and titter, as they passed in the corridor, or bumped into them at the coffee machine. Nothing was articulated, but both Lee and H sensed that words had been said, and they were becoming a laughing stock.

What they guessed had happened—which turned out to be right—was that the CEO, who lacked confidence in the soft issues (and culture was certainly a soft issue) had taken soundings on the concept amongst some of the senior staff. Unfortunately, he had chosen one or two of the most cynical members of his team to confide in, and the reaction was predictable. Word spread fast, and Lee and H became the butt of knowing looks and sniggers, which didn't take long to turn into outright ridicule.

The two colleagues realized it wasn't worth challenging the CEO to come up with a specific response to their proposal. It was dead in the water, and so, to all extents and purposes, were they. This was the set-back they had dreaded, but half expected. At least the lack of decisiveness on the part of the CEO would give them some time to plan their next move.

They met up in Lee's home one weekend to plot what that move might be. Plan B—finding other jobs—was a very viable option, as several calls from headhunters had demonstrated—but both felt so excited by their concept and brand that they felt the need to explore it further.

They felt it was a strong idea, with merit. They had become excited working on the development of the brand and the plan to deliver it, and both felt they would never forgive themselves if they didn't do something with it.

After a long conversation throwing ideas around, they agreed on a course of action. They decided they would resign from the company, and set up in business together as a consultancy, providing delivery programs to organizations for culture improvement. Their company name would be The Value Centrifuge. They felt excited and empowered by the prospect. Fortunately H was a very powerful networker and highly regarded in human resources, across several industry sectors. This meant they would at least get their foot in the door of many potential clients, and would be assured of an attentive hearing.

H insisted that all income, from whatever source, coming into the company should be shared. This was generous, as in the early days it was likely that he would bring in a great deal more clients and income than Lee, who had no reputation in HR, and few contacts. Once in the door, however, Lee's experience in marketing and operations would give great authority to their presentations and programs. Line managers tend to listen to, and believe, other line managers (or ex-line managers) more than they do either consultants or people from non-line functions like HR, simply because they have a more direct responsibility for their recommendations and actions.

The two of them would thus make a persuasive team. The first test of that persuasiveness would lie in their ability to sell the concept to their wives. Both had young families, so the financial risk was not inconsiderable. They were quite high earners, and had a little money put aside, but like most people they tended to spend at least as much as they earned, so no guaranteed monthly pay check would be a new experience. They would be right outside their comfort zones, in a world of risk. If the project failed, and they decided to go back into paid employment, it could still take several months to get the right job; so financial uncertainty was built into the project, whatever happened.

Fortunately the set-up costs would be relatively low, as they decided to work out of their homes, and do their own secretarial work, until the volume of work they attracted justifying committing to such overheads.

After long and concerned discussion, both wives backed the plan. They were fearful of the risks involved, but could see that their husbands had a passion to create value for other people, and a workable plan to deliver the difference they desired to make.

Lee and H set about forming their company, The Value Centrifuge, and prepared to hand in their notice. They realized they would need to redefine their purpose for their new situation. They articulated their new purpose thus:

To transform organizations' cultures by releasing the energies of employees to create more worthwhile value for customers.

This seemed to go some way to capturing the essence of what they were trying to do, which was to give employees a sense of meaning in what they were doing, so they could put more of themselves and their enthusiasm into their jobs. This would directly result in their creating a fairer and more enjoyable customer experience, which in turn would feed back into an enhanced brand reputation, and more job satisfaction for employees. Thus the virtuous value circle would be perpetuated, and the centrifugal force created would throw off value for customers, employees and other stakeholders in the organization concerned.

They already had their concept and their brand, so they now needed to progress to the next step in their Difference Imperative, and update their **stimulus**. This they found harder than expected, as the immediate urgency of their situation in their current employment no longer applied. There was no urgent imperative to turn the tide of cynicism and return the company to positive, life and value-enhancing behaviors. After mulling it over, they came up with the following:

> **The urgent need to emancipate the employees in many organizations from the drudgery of value-neutral or value-reducing work.**

Lee and H resigned, and set out on their adventure. They had the usual setbacks, rejections, and failures that any new enterprise has. They survived them, and went on to grow a successful company that brought great satisfaction to both themselves and their clients. Their sense of personal fulfillment was complete when, some three years later, they got a phone call from P, their colleague from the mobile phone company. After a very successful period as general manager of overseas territories, he had been appointed CEO, in place of the previous incumbent, who was seen as a failure by many of the large shareholders.

P was delighted to catch up with them, and asked that they urgently come in and transform the culture of the company. It was the sweetest of victories, and what made it even more satisfying was that their program was hugely successful, setting the company back on course to being once more an industry leader.

And now let's see what Helen is up to.

HELEN FINDS HER WAY, BUT NOT WITHOUT FINDING A DEAD END OR TWO

Helen spent the next few days planning her course of action. She finally decided to resign before she did anything else. She decided this for several reasons. First, her high salary as a successful corporate lawyer meant she could pay her mortgage and live fairly comfortably for a least a couple of years on the money she had put aside, so absence of income was not an urgent problem for her. Second, the pressure of her job, which frequently involved working extremely long and unsocial hours, would leave her no time to research or plan her future.

A third reason was that she felt an urgent need to start rebuilding her relationships with friends and family—especially with her parents and their new partners. She needed to know she would be available in the evenings and at weekends to do this.

Helen made an appointment with the legal partner she worked for, and handed in her resignation. It caused consternation, because she was very popular with clients, and was a fast and effective worker. The partner worried that she had had some form of breakdown, and offered her time off to get herself back together, but eventually accepted she was of sound mind and serious about her decision to leave the firm. With great reluctance he accepted her resignation, and asked her to finish the merger she was working on, which would take about five or six weeks. This she agreed to do, but in the days and weeks that followed she found it hard to concentrate on the case in hand, because her heart and mind were elsewhere.

She knew she couldn't commit to investing the time that would be required into rebuilding her family relationships until she had left the law practice, so she spent the cracks of time available after her working day in planning her future. She also found time to look up one or two friends, in particular John, her close friend from university. They met one evening in a bar near where she lived. After the usual banter, she broke her news: "I'm resigning from corporate law to become a Difference Driver. I'm going to change the world!"

John looked startled, but when he saw she wasn't joking, jumped to his feet and kissed her. And then hugged her. Before he released her, Helen felt a strange sensation of joy she had not felt in a long time. "What was that about?" she gasped when he released her. "Welcome back to the world, Helen, my dearest, my darling." John was full of joy too. "You've been away too long. We've all got a lot of catching up to do."

They spoke of old times and old friends. They laughed a lot, and Helen went home that evening feeling she really was rejoining the world. The merger she was working on ran into unexpected regulatory problems, so her firm released her three weeks early. Her leaving party was attended by an unusually high number of partners and colleagues, and left her with a good feeling about her firm. Her leaving present from the firm was one of unusual insight and sympathy. It was a gold watch, with no hands or figures, just the words, *carpe diem* inscribed on it. Seizing the day, relishing each moment as it passed, looking for fulfillment now, rather than in some mythical future, was exactly what she intended to do.

Sitting down to plan her life could have been somewhat daunting, but Helen found it a positive and uplifting challenge. She first set about deciding on the domain in which she would make her difference. She felt resignation from work, and the fact that she was in a comfortable position financially, gave her the opportunity to make work the domain in which she would make a difference.

This meant she could become a Beneficial Presence with her family and friends. She reflected that this was a big challenge in itself, as she had been a brooding, and at times even a surly, presence over recent years. She had a great deal of catching up to do, and several bridges to rebuild. Her first step was to ring both her parents, and, to their delight, arrange to spend a weekend with each of them and their new partners.

Thinking hard about her work domain, she wrestled long and hard over whether she should become a Difference Driver or a Difference Deliverer. She had said in jest to her friend John that she would become a Difference Driver, but thinking about it, she wondered whether she could be just as effective at creating value, and making a positive difference to the world, if she became a Difference Deliverer. There were so many worthwhile humanitarian and conservational causes already in existence that she questioned whether she might not be better employed helping one of those forward, rather than partially reinventing the wheel, and starting a new one.

Eventually she cast her mind back to the letter she had written as her supposedly 75-year-old self, and recalled the concept of the charity set up to help people who had fallen into debt. She felt the idea still had merit, and chimed with her desire to help the downtrodden, although it didn't resonate so fully with her wish to help young people. She therefore set about trying to refine her **purpose**, to bring more clarity to what was going to be her future.

After much reflection and several dead ends, she came to define her purpose as follows:

> **To help people to free themselves from the shackles holding them, so they can be free to blossom, and be themselves.**

She realized it wasn't very short and snappy, but it seemed to hit most of her hot buttons. The only one it missed was that she was not specifying young people, rather than people in general, as she felt this might rule out her interest in helping those in debt, many of whom tended to be supporting young families themselves. She felt the idea of shackles inhibiting fulfillment or happiness was an accurate one, as it covered a wide area of human suffering, from those recovering from the mental shackles of trauma of all kinds, to the physical shackles of disabilities or injuries.

Her skills in building people up, and making them feel good about themselves, could come into full play. This, she realized, is what gave her a real buzz. Helping the fallen to rise to their feet was what gave her most satisfaction, and this would become her purpose.

She moved onto her concept, which she took from her letter, feeling it to be the result of a flash of intuition, which still held true some weeks after she had first had it. So she defined her purpose thus:

To create a charity to help those in crippling debt, and to lobby for more responsible marketing of consumer lending.

Helen appreciated that while this was a worthwhile purpose, her knowledge of what the real issues were was somewhat hazy. She therefore decided, before moving on to attempt to **brand** the concept, she would research the area in more depth, to gain a fuller understanding of where the greatest needs lay.

Examining the organizations and charities already operating in the area of debt counseling and litigation resolution, she honed in on a couple that seemed of particular interest and relevance. She therefore decided to divide her week up. She would do volunteer work with each of them for a couple of days a week, and on the fifth day she would research charities working with young people, to see if any of them would cause her to refocus her purpose to include young people.

Helen knew that this last decision wasn't very tidy strategically —indeed it called part of her purpose, as it was currently stated, into question—but she felt that it was so important to get her purpose accurately defined, that keeping her investigations wide at this stage was no bad thing. What she was looking for was some minor epiphany, some flash of insight into her purpose, which in effect would be her **stimulus.**

Six months later Helen's life had progressed significantly, but while she was much further forward, she was also still far from clear on the future pattern of her life. It had not all been plain sailing, and she had needed all her reserves of character and courage at times to see her through. The most positive part of her life was unexpected. She had begun seeing all her friends more often, and had quickly rebuilt her relationships with them. She was seeing her friend John very frequently, and was amazed to find that a strong romantic relationship had developed. John was even more surprised. He had not intended to settle down or get married for several more years yet, and was therefore slightly amazed to find his mind wandering ever more frequently towards such issues.

What had not gone so smoothly was the rebuilding of the relationships with her parents and their partners. Her parents' initial delight at her coming to their various houses for the weekend had been tempered by their partners' reactions, which basically were—not so fast. Neither of them was prepared to let Helen off so lightly for the extended pain she had caused her father and mother by effectively cutting them off. She was building bridges, but it was hard work.

She was, however, beginning to make some progress with her mother and her partner, and things were beginning to look brighter. Her father's partner, on the other hand, was a different matter. While she felt her father was reaching out to her, his partner was digging in, resisting all approaches. Helen got the feeling at times that it wasn't just her that was causing the blockage. There seemed to be something else going on that was upsetting the family dynamics.

After several months, she discovered what this was. Going one weekend to spend time with her father and stepmother, she found her step-sister, a girl of about 20 she had only met a few times, also staying there. From what Helen could remember of her, she had been an outgoing and cheerful girl, but she now seemed enclosed in her own world, and resistant to attempts to engage her in conversation. It did not take Helen long to understand that her stepmother's love for her daughter was profound, but that the difficulties the child was going through were affecting all her relationships, even, she noticed, her relationship with her husband, Helen's father.

Helen, who was very skilled at getting young people to open up, got nowhere with the girl, and ended the weekend with a new respect and sympathy for her stepmother, who was clearly not giving up on her daughter, whatever challenges faced her. She was a Beneficial Presence for her daughter of great tenacity and humanity.

Back at work with her debt counseling volunteer work on the Monday morning, Helen was beginning to worry. Although she found the work worthwhile, she also found the overall experience very challenging. The reason for this, she came to realize, was twofold. First, one of the things she enjoyed doing most was making people feel better, and giving them hope for the future. She found this very difficult to do with many of the people she was counseling, because she couldn't in all honesty give them too much hope.

Time and again she found the administration of the law erratic in the way it adjudicated on the matters of debt, so her hopes were frequently dashed too. She felt that financial institutions were abusing vulnerable individuals (possibly unwittingly—she wasn't sure how much they really understood of the impact of their behavior), and the law was fickle in how it defended them. When mistakes were made in the allocation of interest repayments or penalties, the credit card companies and banks were impossibly slow to acknowledge them—if they ever did—and used their financial muscle to leverage the law to their maximum benefit.

The second reason for her disquiet was her slow realization that possibly she was not a very good tilter at windmills. While the idea of fighting the credit card companies and other lenders appealed to her intellectually, she got a black feeling in her stomach each time she considered actually taking them on. She understood rationally that spending the next 10 or 20 years of her life taking on financial institutions would create huge value for many people who desperately needed that value. But for her, frankly, it was a dispiriting thought. She knew she ought to relish it, but she found the thought filled her with profound gloom.

She worried about this. It did not sit comfortably with either her idea of herself, or the purpose she had defined for herself. She was reluctantly coming to the conclusion that debt counseling and fighting the consumer institutions was beginning to paralyze her spirit, rather than fire her with enthusiasm. Had she chosen the wrong purpose, or was this the beginning of a failure of courage on her part? Should she fight on through this difficult period, so she could emerge victorious freeing the unfairly oppressed from unjustified debt?

After much reflection—and finally discussion with John—she came to the conclusion it was the former. She knew enough about herself to be confident that it was not a failure of courage. She had character and courage aplenty. What she was facing was a misdefinition of purpose. Rather than receiving energy and enthusiasm from fulfilling her purpose, she was finding a dwindling of energy, and a dread at the thought of carrying on the work.

What finally confirmed her in this view was watching several of her colleagues at the organization and the charity she did her volunteering work for. They were doing just the work defined in her purpose. They were counseling people in debt with great skill, and they were lobbying hard with the government to amend the law to better control consumer lending, and the financial institutions to improve their behavior. They relished the fight, and were fired up to take on all comers.

The challenge clearly excited them, but it de-energized her. She concluded from this that it must be her current purpose that was wrong for her, rather than a deficit of courage. If her purpose was wrongly defined, and was not truly motivating for her, no amount of courage would replace the energy and enthusiasm deficit.

As she pondered on the implications of her conclusions, she continued with her volunteer work, to give herself time to rethink her situation. A few weeks later, she was working her day with a young persons' charity, which she found she was enjoying more and more. She was dividing her time between two charities, doing a day a fortnight with each.

The first charity she worked for was one involved in raising money for street children in Africa. The stories of the children's suffering moved her deeply, but as the children themselves were located on another continent, her work involved money raising and publicity activity to raise awareness of the children's plight, rather than helping the children individually. She had no opportunity to be a Beneficial Presence to any of the street kids.

The second charity focused on young women who had been through trauma. This covered a depressingly wide spectrum of abuse—sexual abuse by family members; FGM (female genitalia mutilation); acid attacks from jealous ex-husbands, or deposed wives; exploitation of asylum seekers by unprincipled employers; ostracism for adultery (while the male adulterers went scot-free); exploitation in prostitution, and much more.

The traumatized women came from all backgrounds and situations. Many just happened to have been in the wrong place at the wrong time. One Friday Helen met the administrator, a large and unwaveringly cheerful woman, who talked to her about the girl she would be helping that day. "This girl's been through it," she said. "She took occasional drugs at school, but got heavily into drugs on her gap year before university—fell in with the wrong set, traveling in South America. She hit bottom, got into prostitution to survive, but eventually got home 18 months ago. She's been through rehab, and seems to be staying off the drugs. The trauma is still there. The psychiatrists have had several sessions with her, and she seems to be making progress. She goes home at weekends, but still finds it difficult to cope. The doctor in charge feels a session or two with someone like you could be a very useful next step."

The administrator smiled, and led Helen down the corridor, opened a door, and ushered her in. "Jane, this is Helen. Helen—Jane." With another broad smile, she turned on her heel, and left. Helen and Jane looked at each other, and both had an involuntary intake of breath.

Jane was Helen's step-sister, her father's wife's daughter from her first marriage. "Wow," said Helen, after a long pause, "The ethics of this dictate that I can't talk to you in this environment—you being family. All I can say is that I've had the whole briefing on your case, and I can't unlearn that. What I can assure you is it won't go further than the two of us."

She paused, reluctant to leave her so abruptly. "I've made a few mistakes myself, Jane, and done things I wish I hadn't, so I suspect we've quite a bit in common. If you like to just chat sometime, away from here, I'd love to share some of them with you. Do feel free to call, any time. Here's my mobile number."

She scribbled the number on a piece of paper lying on the table, then smiled, took Jane briefly by the arms, kissed her on the cheeks, and left the room. She explained the situation to the administrator, who said, "Pity. Right decision though. I'll find you someone else."

Helen hoped against hope that Jane would take up her offer to call her. She had been deeply touched by Jane's story before meeting her, and, in the brief moments they had spent together before she'd had to withdraw, had warmed to her as a person in a way that she could not have guessed from the awkward meeting at her father's house. Perhaps it was knowing her story, or perhaps she was in less defensive mode, expecting to open up to someone. Whatever it was, it gave Helen a strong appetite to be of help, if she possibly could be.

It was 10 days later that Jane called. She said she wanted to explain a few things. They met in a quiet coffee shop near the house. Before Jane could launch into anything, Helen managed to engage her in small talk about what was going on in the world, and in the family. Within a quarter of an hour, Jane was laughing. Helen had been telling a story, in which she imitated her father's voice in stern, telling-off mode. It made them both laugh, because he was basically a warm, humorous man, not made for sternness, and he wasn't very good at it. He found it difficult to sustain the mood, and frequently finished off with his voice rapidly rising, as he fought to suppress a giggle. This was the note Helen caught, perfectly.

Taking Helen's lead, Jane began to open up with family small talk. They chatted on, until Helen realized her parking meter was running out of time. They rose, kissed goodbye, and agreed to meet the following week. They met frequently after that. They enjoyed meeting, enjoying many laughs together. Jane's traumatic experiences were never mentioned, and soon dropped into the past for both of them. Jane knew she could trust Helen, and Helen knew she had a step-sister who was developing once more into a warm and friendly human being.

After the first few meetings, and more work with the charity, Helen redefined her purpose thus:

To help traumatized young women to free themselves of their trauma, so they can blossom as human beings.

Interestingly, Helen had been on a journey from Difference Driver, to Difference Deliverer, to Beneficial Presence. As a would-be changer of debt law and moneylender behavior, she had been a Difference Driver. As a fundraiser and publicist for the street child charity, she had been a Difference Deliverer, and as a counselor with the trauma charity, she had been a Beneficial Presence.

As a Beneficial Presence, Helen had found her concept, and indeed, in the specific charity she found most fulfillment in, she had found her brand. Her stepsister Jane was her initial stimulus, but she found plenty of other girls after that to sustain a very high level of motivation.

She began to work five days a week at the young women's charity, mixing marketing, legal, and fundraising activity in with her counseling work with the girls. Her challenge became to retain her counseling work—which she loved—because the charity came to rely more and more on her leadership and revenue-generating skills to build its presence, and their partnerships, throughout the world.

She was thus Beneficial Presence to trauma sufferers part of the week, and Difference Deliverer for the rest of the week. She was now certain she had found her true purpose. She had her stimulus in the daily meeting with abused and suffering girls and women. The concept was accurately and ably delivered by the charity she worked for. And the brand, like the concept, was also supplied by the charity she was now helping to build.

A year later, Helen married John. Her mother and father came to the wedding with their respective partners, and all got on very well. Jane was Helen's maid of honor, and it was a very happy day. Helen and John went on to have three lovely children. Things were going swimmingly until John had a bad car accident, and was incapacitated. He was unable to work, so

Jane, as well as being a superb Beneficial Presence to him, became the only breadwinner.

By then, the charity—greatly helped by Helen's competence and enthusiasm—had become large enough to pay her as the professional manager she was, so they had enough money to survive on.

For Helen, the choice between the financial wealth she would have enjoyed as a corporate lawyer, and the wealth of fulfillment she enjoyed as a mother, wife, daughter, and life changer, was not worth a moment's consideration. Jane became a great friend (as did Helen's stepmother), and subsequently joined the charity to help bring to others the release from trauma she had found there.

Helen, like Lee, had found her purpose, and had found the concept, the brand, and the stimulus to fulfill and sustain that purpose. She had created relevant value for the young women trauma sufferers, and for all of them, she had made a huge difference.

10

So where do we go from here?

Everyone can be great. Because anyone can serve. You don't have to have a college degree to serve. You don't have to make your subject and your verb agree to serve. You don't have to know about Plato and Aristotle to serve. You don't have to know about Einstein's theory of relativity to serve. You don't have to know about the second theory of thermodynamics in physics to serve. You only need a heart full of grace and a soul generated by love.

Martin Luther King

The purpose of this book is to help the growing number of us who are seeking a more fulfilling life to map the territory of how we can be more effective at making a difference. In so doing we can realize more of our potential as human beings. As we have seen, more and more of us are already volunteering our help, but many of us want to do so using our skills to deliver more meaningful and relevant outputs. The book sets out to help us understand our purpose better, and direct our energies and enthusiasms better, so we can be more effective in our goal of making a difference.

Before drawing some overall conclusions, let's look again at some of the core concepts of the book. This will enable us both to refresh our memories on what those concepts were, and to see them in the wider perspective of their possible role in society.

Central to the book is the concept of the Make a Difference Mindset, which enables us to develop competence to ensure that difference making is a deliberate, conscious skill that positively improves situations, relationships, lives, and societies.

It creates an inner confidence that we can deliver the difference we decide to make.

Categorizing ourselves as Difference Drivers (passionate antagonists of the status quo on a specific issue), Difference Deliverers (who help make change happen), or Beneficial Presences (who are the positive, healing difference) helps us define how radical, or otherwise, we intend to be.

There is, of course, overlap between the categories. Mahatma Gandhi was a case in point, who crossed the divide. He was a Beneficial Presence of such power, with values and beliefs of such clarity and effectiveness, that he became a profound Difference Driver. His personal example helped spread his philosophy of non-violent resistance, and was potent enough to topple the British domination of India, which had lasted for over a century.

The Mindset itself does not exist in a vacuum. The societal context is highly relevant.

Our rise in affluence and the consequent progress up Maslow's hierarchy of needs seems to be giving us a greater desire to serve others. Not only are we getting more satisfaction and fulfillment out of giving service, but also there is a parallel, and probably related, trend for a feeling of optimism to overcome pessimism.

Despite the best efforts of postmodernism, and the perpetrators of the Myth of Decline, more and more of us are feeling good about our personal situation. This is accompanied by a feeling of greater responsibility towards others less fortunate than ourselves.

This is confirmed by a recent Sociovision study, which shows our personal optimism to be high (58 percent of us feeling personally optimistic, versus 9 percent feeling pessimistic), while at the same time fearing for the future of society as a whole (only 23 percent optimistic, and 43 percent pessimistic). It is this sense of personal optimism, coupled with a growing sense of personal responsibility—the need to get involved as an individual—that is the fertile ground in which the Make a Difference Mindset can flourish.

For optimists everything is possible. Because they are positive people, they take responsibility, and are first in line to hold their hands up to volunteer to make things better. This in itself creates a virtuous circle of the improvements (the differences) they make feeding back into their own self-esteem and self-fulfillment. This in turn makes them healthier, more confident, and more likely to continue to create relevant value for others in the future.

Evidence is even emerging that volunteering keeps you young. Numerous studies have revealed that volunteering into old age enhances both physical and psychological health, and lowers rates of depression and mortality. Yes, making a difference for other people actually makes you happier, and you live longer.

Moving on to the architecture of the Make a Difference Mindset, the foundations for the edifice is the discovery of our purpose.

Having a purpose removes at a stroke one of the major causes of depression—considered by some to be one of the major killer diseases of the twenty-first century—because it gives us a cogent reason for existing.

As human beings, having a purpose—understanding that our lives have meaning—sets us apart from other animals. We want to feel part of something bigger than ourselves.

Finding the defining thread that runs through and meaningfully connects our often-random experiences is not a quick job. Some know their purpose from childhood, but for most of us we need to tease it out, treating it as a major project in our lives, until we can feel confident we can articulate it, or, more importantly, *feel* it in every fiber of our being.

This can be tantalizing in the extreme to achieve. It sounds so simple and obvious, but, as we respond with compassion to different stimuli at different times in our lives, we can find conflicting messages as to the exact definition of our purpose. This should not be a cause for concern. Most of us aren't predestined to be doctors or teachers. Our purpose just isn't written in the stars from birth.

We have a general desire to help others, but need to work at focusing it. **The Values Map**, the obituaries from various people near to us, and the letter to a young friend written from the perspective of our having reached 75 or so years of age, all help us to gain greater insight into how we can best serve our fellow human beings.

The Values Map gives us our magnetic north—the general direction in which our fulfillment lies. Crystallizing our purpose gives us the true north—the area of activity in which we will find our true meaning.

Once we are on the way to better understanding our purpose, we need to work on becoming **captains of our souls**, so we can rise to the challenges that will inevitably face us as we set out to fulfill our purpose, and make a difference. We must eschew the deterministic comfort blanket, and take responsibility for our attitudes, behavior, values, hopes, and courage. We finally grow up, are accountable for our actions, and we stop blaming others for our shortcomings.

Character is not just taking responsibility for what we do. It's also taking responsibility for who we are as well.

This involves our persona as well as our character. Both character and persona are involved in our personal development, but we understand that the former underpins the latter, and on its own, persona is fragile, and liable to break down under pressure. When we behave as ourselves in all situations, we make sure our integrity is not compromised. We avoid the stress that is the direct result of being different people, according to circumstances, and our subconscious is not put under unbearable pressure by our behaving with one set of ethical standards at work, and a different set at home with our families.

We understand, in Oscar Wilde's phrase, that every action of the common day makes and unmakes character. We listen to our **conscience**, which is the litmus test for our integrity, and an unerring guide to the right way to behave. It tells us what is fair, or what is unfair, what is kind, or what is hurtful, and what is true, or what is false.

To character and conscience, we then need to add courage.

When we know what we stand for, and have a worthy purpose, we can't be totally private about it. At some time we will have to stand up and be counted. This is where courage comes in.

Character and courage move us from passive to active.

They help us survive in situations where resilience and perseverance are demanded. We are no longer children, looking round for help from grown-ups. We are fully fledged adults, taking responsibility for the difference we intend to make.

Making that difference is essentially creating new, or relevant, value for the particular issue, domain, or person, we have selected to focus our energies on to fulfill our purpose. This value may be the simple (but not easy) act of providing unconditional love for a troubled family member (and making them feel valued). Or it may be the establishment of consistent, and enforced, standards of behavior, to provide a sense of security for confused or rebellious children—or even work colleagues—based on an understood and agreed framework of fairness and justice.

Alternatively, the value you intend to create may, like Bob Hunter, co-founder of Greenpeace, lie in exposing dangerous and unthinking behavior by governments, organizations, or individuals. By bringing pressure to bear, you may be able to change that behavior, and in so doing improve the quality of life for single individuals or whole societies. Preventing abuse by the powerful is an excellent way to create value.

Good leadership, too, is a strong creator of value.

Painting the bigger picture, giving meaning to everyday activity, helps us all, as toiling stonemasons, play our part in creating great architecture of social and even spiritual worth.

Good leaders are intrinsically difference makers.

They create value, not just by changing and improving things, but also by building up their followers to become leaders themselves. Focusing on how they can serve their followers, rather than on what they can get out of them, they create a wide ripple effect of value.

The effects of good leadership are magnified by changing economic structures. Because human talent and ideas are now the chief drivers of economic value and wealth, rather than raw materials and capital, a strong individual with a good idea can create unprecedented value. Muhammad Yunus was a case in point. In conceiving and building the Grameen Bank and its subsequent offshoots, he has created previously unimaginable opportunity for the poor of Bangladesh—especially for the women who take up 94 percent of the loans, and have become the family breadwinners.

The next step in the process of honing the skills needed to be an effective Difference Driver, or Difference Deliverer, is the choice of the domain in which we want to make an impact.

This can be anything from sport, to music, work, family, society, or whatever. The range is wide. The important thing is to choose one that aligns with our purpose, and focus all efforts on that (although being a Beneficial Presence in another domain at the same time is feasible and worthwhile).

Once the domain is finalized, the Difference Imperative kicks in.

The Difference Imperative adds the power of a specific stimulus to our purpose. That stimulus is a supercharge of emotion we can call upon to give us passion and energy to create new value. It may be an imagined state (like being Olympic champion in sport, or winning an international competition in music) or a mental picture of human suffering from a specific disease, type of pollution, abuse, and so on, or even the individuals suffering from the status quo we are determined to change.

Whatever stimulus we choose, its role is to set the pulses racing again when the going gets difficult, and the enthusiasm for the difference we want to drive or deliver is beginning to wane. Whatever our courage and perseverance, whatever the power of our purpose, there are times when results seem slow in coming, and resistance to our efforts seems overwhelming. Being able to call up our specific stimulus at these times can redouble our commitment. Seeing a mental picture of the reason we are fighting—our cause, if you like—makes quitting an impossibility. It gives us fresh energy to carry on, till we finally achieve the difference we are seeking to drive or deliver.

Once our purpose and stimulus are in place, the next step in the Difference Imperative is to evolve a concept capable of creating sufficient value to change the situation for the better.

The quality of the concept (the input) will equal the quality of the output (how effective it is in making the positive difference we seek). The concept should be as radical and imaginative as possible. The more daring and exciting the idea, the more likely it is to capture imaginations, move hearts, and change situations.

To give the concept depth and color, so it sticks in people's minds, it may be appropriate to make it into a brand.

Of course, you can't create instant brands, but you can put the elements in place, so that over time, as you build trust by being consistently trustworthy, you have half a chance of building something worthwhile and enduring. Brands like Greenpeace and Amnesty are now up there with famous grocery brands like Coca-Cola in terms of recognition and trust.

Even if your brand is of short-term duration, the disciplines in thinking through the concept in terms of creating a brand may be extremely beneficial. It is, however, only worth thinking in terms of creating a brand if your concept is robust to start with. If it isn't robust, you may get short-term support on a personal sympathy vote from people who know you and love you, but in the longer term the concept will need solid and wide appeal, if it is to have any legs.

Brands, however diverse the product or service field they operate in, have a simple essence. Sony for instance, covers music, technology, computer games, and heaven knows what, but you still have a clear understanding of Sony's brand essence. It is about product quality, innovation, excitement, but above all, it is a cool brand. It is cool not just in the sense of being plugged in and up to the moment, but in the more important sense of being respected for what it is.

It doesn't try too hard to be "with it." It has a self-confidence and a sense of humor that gives it that inner nod from consumers, because most people see it as a friend. It may come and go in terms of performance on the stock market, but it has that inner integrity which means it could perform very badly for a long time and still be forgiven when it came back in its true colors of a high-quality, innovative, fun brand—a brand that is good to be around, and have around.

The concept, and the subsequent branding we come up with, is unlikely to have the richness and variety of a Sony. It can, however, in the same way as Sony, know clearly what it stands for and what sort of reputation it seeks to build. It can make our concept readily understood and communicated.

It can excite minds, and create energy.

Most importantly, it can create a rallying focus for activity for the Difference Deliverers.

Many of the differences that need to be created are slow, and even difficult to explain and communicate to people. Think of the organizations that were started by Difference Drivers, and were made effective by Difference Deliverers: Amnesty International, Greenpeace—as we've already seen—Médicins Sans Frontières, Boy Scouts and Girl Guides, Oxfam, and the Red Cross, to name but a few.

Then ask yourself two questions. The first question is: could you explain to someone the value these operations bring to people around the world in less than half a dozen words (against the one, or two, in the brand name)? The brand name communicates the cause and the benefits it brings (the difference it makes) with a brevity impossible if the brand did not exist. The brand, with its reputation and its values, distils many layers of heritage and meaning into a simple logo and name.

The second question is: do you think the workers within the organizations could operate as effectively with governments, NGOs, and all the many interfaces with which they have to interact in order to be able to deliver their benefits, if they did not have the strength of the brand—with all its heritage and trustworthiness—behind them? The brand is their calling card. It enables them to short-circuit and overcome innumerable obstacles that would otherwise be put in their way to slow them down, and possibly prevent them from carrying on their good work.

The brand also provides reassurance and trust for donors.

When natural disasters occur, there are always stories of funds being misappropriated before they reach the sufferers who desperately need them. Because they have been through a long and steep learning curve in this key area of operation, the major brands now know, to a high degree, how to evade the corrupt intermediaries and funds diverters. They ensure that the money you give not only reaches its destination, but also is spent effectively.

So brands speed communication, open doors that otherwise might remain shut, and, over time, learn how to deploy funds and activity effectively. Brands like the ones mentioned above take a long time to build, but once built, can create value for their beneficiaries with a speed and efficiency that would be extremely hard to come near if the brand did not exist.

The final step in the Difference Imperative is making it happen.

If you want to become a Difference Driver or a Difference Deliverer you may have specific goals. Then again, you may not—preferring to let your purpose and stimulus-driven enthusiasm carry you through. Either way is good. What is vital, though, is that you have a delivery date on it. Being accountable comes with the territory of being serious about making a difference.

THE NEED AND THE DESIRE TO MAKE A DIFFERENCE

We live in a world that is increasingly fluid, unpredictable, exciting, messy, and vulnerable. The multiplicity of media now available to us daily exposes us to abuses, suffering, successes and opportunities, all intermingled.

Despite rapid change and the dissolving of the old certainties, many of us feel a rising sense of optimism. We feel a growth of inner confidence, and of hope. We sense a need to respond to situations, whether they are in our own homes, places of work or further afield in our communities or elsewhere on the planet. These situations may be very positive—like the opportunity to excel in our chosen domain of sport, the arts, or teaching, for example. They may, alternatively, be situations where other human beings' behavior—or an accident of nature—has brought about the need for urgent corrective action.

The *need* for people to add value, improve situations, and make a difference is huge. What is new about the world today—especially in the developed world, where affluence (rising incomes, stable employment, cheap credit, low prices, and the saturation of basic durables, including mobile phones) is more widely spread—is that there is also a desire to help.

The origins of this desire may be debatable, but that it exists is not.

Quantitative and qualitative research abounds to validate the desire to make a difference. The growth in volunteering is further evidence of the deep yearning to make the world a better place.

The most likely source of this growing desire to help, and to serve, is the affluence-driven growth of independent-minded individualism. The "I" in the title of this book gives us a clue. The "I" is relevant on two dimensions. First, the growth in the drive for personal fulfillment underpins the desire to serve. In a memorable phrase, the Future Foundation, commenting on research showing this growing push for self-actualization, stated it simply: "Consumers do want spiritual sex." Our spirituality—often manifested in giving service to other human beings—gives us a high level of personal satisfaction, as part and parcel of our altruism.

The second dimension on which the "I" is relevant is that of our desire to leave a legacy. The mega rich can buy their legacies. They are able to endow hospitals, universities, art galleries, or charitable foundations. For the rest of us, relatively affluent, but by no means rich, let alone mega-rich, we need to earn our legacies, by making a difference that may live on in the hearts of others, after we have passed on.

So both the need for value to be created, and the desire to create value, are together growing in happy synchronicity. What is less happy is that the need is unlikely ever to be matched by the actions that flow from the desire. There are more people needing help in the world than there are people willing and desirous to give help. Hence the need for us to be more structured and disciplined in our approach to making a difference, to which this book, I hope, is a small contribution.

USING THE INTERROGATIVE IMPERATIVE ON OURSELVES

My wife Lizzie, like many partners, sometimes uses what I call the Interrogative Imperative. When, for instance, friends come round for lunch or supper, she asks me questions like, or "Does more bread need cutting?" "Do we need more salad?" or "Do you think we need coffee?"

It poses as a question, but is in reality an order. It is a gentle form of code, a kind way of saying, "Get off your backside, and do this—now."

Applying this to the Make a Difference Mindset, we can put to ourselves the following questions:

Do I need to identify my high octane, gut-felt values?

Do I need to crystallize and understand my purpose?

Do I need to select my domain?

Do I need to build depth of character, developing courage and conscience?

Do I need to select a motivating stimulus?

Do I need to identify the relevant value I will build into a compelling concept?

Do I need to start building a brand for rapid, positive, emotional connection?

Do I need to set a date to do it by?

Hidden within the questions will be the urgent imperative: yes—and **do it now.**

The one major question that needs to be answered, of course, is whether to be a Beneficial Presence, a Difference Driver, or a Difference Deliverer.

Questions, questions. They are all important, because they are all part of the Make a Difference Mindset architecture. The key question, however, comes back once again to how clear and how compelling your purpose is. Finding the golden thread of purpose, which gives meaning and significance to all your efforts, is the foundation for all other activity.

The quality of the difference we succeed in making will correlate both with the intensity of our purpose, and with the satisfaction we get out of fulfilling it. It's a two-way street.

Lee, our hero of earlier chapters, who worked with his colleague H to create The Value Centrifuge, succeeded in helping organizations rediscover their purpose and find meaning in the work they were doing. To each new client, he gave a spinning top with his logo on. He would spin the top, and say: "This is what we can achieve together. The still center of the top is the calm and certainty you will get from discovering your true purpose. The spinning at the exterior is the almost effortless energy true purpose will generate. And spinning off that, centrifugally, is the new value we will create for all your organization's stakeholders. The potential is in our hands. Let's spin the top, and grasp it together."

Helen, our heroine who regained her life balance, was given a watch by her colleagues at the law firm she resigned from which did not tell the time, but merely said *carpe diem*—seize the day. Helen wore it every day thereafter, to remind herself to take joy now and to strive each hour to fulfill her potential.

The eyes for the face my daughter had drawn were still in her pencil. We need to take the next step and act decisively now, to move our good intentions into effective actions. In so doing, we will draw a face on the page of our personal history that will both fulfill our potential, and truly make a difference.

Bibliography

Richard Barrett, *Liberating the Corporate Soul: Building a visionary organisation*, Butterworth Heinemann, Boston, Mass, 1998.

Kevin Cashman, *Leadership from the Inside Out: Becoming a leader for life*, TCLG/Executive Excellence Publishing, 1999, www.eep.com

Jim Collins, *Good to Great*, Random House, London, 2001.

Stephen R. Covey, *The Seven Habits of Highly Effective People*, Prentice Hall, USA, 1993.

Joseph Jaworski, *Synchronicity: The inner path of leadership*, Berrett Koehler, San Francisco, 1998.

Charles Leadbeater, *Up the Down Escalator: Why the global pessimists are wrong*, Penguin, London, 2004.

Anthony O'Hear, *Philosophy in the New Century*, Continuum International, London, 2002.

David Schwartz, *The Magic of Thinking Big*, Simon and Schuster, New York, 1987.

Richard Wilkinson, *The Impact of Inequality: How to make sick societies healthier*, New Press, New York, 2005.

Michael Wilmott and William Nelson, *Complicated Lives: The malaise of modernity*, Wiley, Chichester, 2005, www.wiley.com